A POCKETFUL OF
DYNAMITE

A POCKETFUL OF DYNAMITE

Ellen Wilkie
with Judith Gunn

HODDER & STOUGHTON
LONDON SYDNEY AUCKLAND TORONTO

Cover photograph by David Hevey.

British Library Cataloguing in Publication Data

Wilkie, Ellen, *1958–1989*
  A pocketful of dynamite.
  1. Muscular dystrophic persons – Biographies
  I. Title   II. Gunn, Judith
  362.196748092

  ISBN 0-340-51293-8

To my parents

Acknowledgments

Acknowledgment is gratefully made for permission to include extracts from the *Daily Mail*, the *Daily Telegraph*, the *Independent*, and the *Leicester Mercury*.

Acknowledgment is also gratefully made to Jeremy Grayson for permission to include his photograph of Ellen Wilkie with *Pithy Poems*, and to Channel 4 for use of their photograph of the presenters of *Same Difference*.

Every effort has been made to trace copyright holders of material included in this book. Should appropriate acknowledgments not have been made, the publishers offer sincere apologies.

'I'd rather feel the earth beneath my feet' © Paul Simon, 1970. By kind permission of Pattern Music Ltd.

'My life is changing in so many ways' © Neil Young. By kind permission of Warner Chappell Music Ltd.

'The Long and Winding Road' © John Lennon/Paul McCartney, 1970. Reproduced by kind permission of Northern Songs/EMI Music, London WC2H 0EA.

'I've been on the road so long my friend' © Paul Simon, 1970. By kind permission of Pattern Music Ltd.

'History Lesson' © Steve Turner, 1980. *Up to Date*, Hodder & Stoughton Publishers.

Introduction

Recently I got a letter from my old maths teacher, now vice-head. She wanted to do something about my achievements in school assembly. It would make a boring assembly. Anybody could do what I've done. I don't know what's got into people recently. One of my lecturers said I'd be a perfect person to write a biography about. My dad told me to keep some unimportant letter because 'I might want to write a book one day'. Who does he think I am? The Queen?

1

'I'd rather feel the earth beneath my feet'
Paul Simon

When I was eighteen months old my parents were told that I could not be expected to survive my teens and that I would certainly be in a wheelchair by the time I was ten. I could still walk when I was fourteen and although I am in a wheelchair now, I have to confess to having left my twentieth birthday well behind me. The diagnosis that led to such a bleak outlook for me was Duchenne muscular dystrophy, but even that has not been fully accepted by some of the doctors who have examined me subsequently.

Recently I crossed swords with someone from the Muscular Dystrophy Group on the subject of my diagnosis. When I informed this individual that I had Duchenne muscular dystrophy she replied cheerfully, 'You can't have or you'd be dead.' She went on, 'Only seven women in the world have it and we know about all of them.'

I replied, 'Maybe there are eight.'

'When did you last see a specialist?' she asked, informing me, as if her own tests were definitive, that if I did not need turning in the night, feeding or other personal help, I could not have Duchenne muscular dystrophy. 'Maybe that's because I had medication and went swimming a lot.'

'There are some very good tests these days. Why

don't you have the test? It would put your mind at rest.'

'No, it wouldn't. It wouldn't make any difference. Are all seven women dead, then?'

'Yes, er, no, but they will be by their late teens.' Perhaps she thought she was talking to a ghost.

Duchenne muscular dystrophy is a muscle-wasting disease which makes you progressively weaker. The problem with this diagnosis for me was that I am female and Duchenne muscular dystrophy is only supposed to occur in males. It is normally an inherited disease, but there was no trace of it in my family on either side. I have a lot of male relatives and because it is hereditary, it should have occurred in one of them – but it didn't. In fact, this type of muscular dystrophy does occur in females but it is very, very rare. At the last count, as the specialist noted, there were eight of us (including me) in the world, so my having the disease is literally a chance almost in a hundred million. I seem to be some sort of mutant – typical Ellen, determined to be different. This, of course, was why doctors disputed (and some still do) that I have Duchenne muscular dystrophy.

One of the earliest medical tests I had involved taking blood from my earlobe in order to establish whether or not I really was a girl and not just a boy in disguise. The test proved me to be a female and it is not something that I or my family have ever doubted. I was terrified at the prospect of the test, not realising it was just a little needle. I thought it would be a lot of big machines drawing blood out of me. I made a real fuss so my parents said, 'If you're good we'll buy you a monkey.' I wasn't very good but I still got a monkey. He had wire arms, legs and tail so he clung on to me – he was my favourite toy. Another test, a muscle biopsy, literally hamstrung me at the age of three. A piece of the muscle was taken from the back of my leg. With two stitches in my leg, I walked on tiptoe because it hurt too much to put my foot down flat. I was only a toddler at the time. The tendon shortened and I ended up permanently on tiptoe on that foot. I suppose I should have had intensive physiotherapy. This round of medical attention and tests confirmed that I did have Duchenne muscular dystrophy. The neurologist remarked, 'I've never seen it so advanced in one so young,' so the prognosis was grim.

I can't remember a particular time when I realised I had muscular dystrophy. I do remember that I did a lot of things sitting down when I was small. My uncle, who was a surgeon, gave the first real clue to my parents that there was something wrong. He noticed that when I was being bathed with my cousin (of the same age, about two and a half) I hauled myself out of the bath in a way that he thought looked dystrophic. For referral to a paediatrician, my mother took me to our G.P. who pointed out that it could be a dislocated hip, a common problem in young children. But my uncle was right and Duchenne dystrophy was pronounced.

From the outset, my parents' policy was to bring me up as an ordinary child with a normal family background (though I'm not sure if our family's exactly normal) and a standard education, which seemed to surprise everyone. Early advice from one G.P. was that I should be put in an institution because of the possible adverse effect on my brothers. I think my presence did have an effect – a very profound and good effect – judging from the way they have all turned out. Of course none of us were angels. We used to fight and one older brother kept pushing me and my little brother around. The youngest, Alcuin, sometimes complained about carrying me and pretended to drop me, or he pushed me round corners on one wheel of my pushchair while I screamed. But he never went too far. He would tease me and say 'you stupid cripple' but he could do it because he was my brother. Some things were hurtful but no more than anything between other brothers and sisters when the teasing got out of hand. Now, all three are certainly very caring, considerate men and the fact that they did have to do those things for me, although they probably didn't like it at the time, was good for us all. One of my brothers is now a psychiatrist,

13

another a fashion designer and the other an agricultural-
ist. I don't think they or my family regret that I stuck
around throughout our childhoods.

The fact that I did stick around, not only as an active
family member to whom no concessions were made (I
did the washing up and laid the table like everybody
else) but also survived my teens, was probably due to
an experimental treatment I was given from the age of
six.

The first dose of Laevadosin was given to me in hospital. It was my first experience of staying in a ward and I
don't recall it all that fondly. For a start, my pyjamas got
lost and I was shoved into a men's pair which upset me
because I liked to have my own identity. They were far
too big for me and I hated the stripes and wanted my own
little brushed nylon ones that Mummy had made for me.
I sat in these huge pyjamas with folded up sleeves, just
not feeling like me. Even my favourite seal brooch,
pinned on my pyjamas, got lost in the wash.

The Laevadosin was administered to me through a
drip, so I had to eat my meals in bed instead of with the
other children at the table. It was very painful when the
tube for the drip was shoved into my arm. I also hated
having sugar on my cornflakes, it was far too sweet, but I
was scared to open my mouth in that great big ward and
say so. I kept hoping someone would ask if I wanted the
sugar, or simply not give it to me. Life on the ward was
not exactly peaceful: I was woken in the night to have my
temperature taken, and during the day one of my fellow
patients, a diabetic girl, took to screaming loudly when
she wasn't allowed ice cream. One happier moment was
when every person in my class at school sent me a card,
done in wax crayons. There were about thirty-six and
they all arrived in one parcel.

Despite the trauma of staying in hospital, my father
noted an improvement in my condition. He wrote to the
British Medical Journal to testify to the fact that my walking, feeding and writing had all improved and that by
that Easter I had refused to wear the caliper on my leg.

14

'Early in the summer holidays,' my father wrote, 'she disappeared, to return later having triumphantly walked round the block alone (circa three hundred yards).'

This improvement was the result of regularly administered doses of the drug. After my visit to the hospital it became possible to give me Laevadosin in the form of an injection in my backside, three times a week. It gave a whole new meaning to the phrase 'a pain in the bum'. The size of the dose was 10 ml., two teaspoons' full, and it did have side effects. It's a stimulant and makes the heart race; it could also make me sick if given too quickly. When I first came home the District Nurse came to give the injection, but she was busy and in her hurry did it so quickly that I nearly fainted. So my father learned the technique, practising on a piece of bacon for hours. In fact, the injections could take anything up to an hour to administer with minimal pain, and in the early days my mother would read to me to take my mind off things – we got through a lot of books that way. Alcuin remembers those stories fondly as he listened in when the family was – how shall I put it – 'gathered round the injected buttock'.

In later years (the injections went on until my early twenties) when I might be late back from a party, my father would occasionally fall asleep over the needle and I would have to wake him up. If I went on holiday without my parents I had to have the injections every day for the week before I went.

As time went by, it became increasingly difficult to find a space in my flesh that had not been too damaged by years of injections to admit the Laevadosin easily. But the belief that the injections probably did stop my disability from worsening in the way that was expected made it worthwhile. Because I kept my strength for such a long time, more tests were done to see if I really had got Duchenne muscular dystrophy. The attitude was 'the diagnosis must be wrong' rather than 'perhaps the injections are working'. However, I still kept on with the injections although I never got used to them. I had to

15

train myself not to tense up, otherwise it hurt all the more. But in all those years of regular injections, three times a week, I was only sick a couple of times which I think is a pretty good record.

I was born and brought up in Bristol. In my early childhood I could still walk. I used to do gym and dance. Even when I couldn't walk I still carried on with dance, of sorts. I became weaker very gradually over a long period of time. I would think about something and realise that I couldn't do it any more. That's how the fact of my disability came home to me. Now, when I think about the time I could walk, I can't imagine how I ever did it. However, I can still walk in water. I go swimming regularly in London and shortly after I started I wrote to my boyfriend: 'Wow! What progress! Four widths with ease but more importantly what strength, what power, to feel and see myself moving, a master of the waters, such confidence. A vast improvement from even the week before.'

Walking on Water

only ask me to live with you in water
or on the moon
and I'll be your dancing partner all year long
queen of my once a week domain
I relive my previous walking
toe-heel, toe-heel, toe-heel
all the blissful width of the pool
a liquid life brings me alive
with balletic sweeps
swinging in the watery freedom
which air denies
graceful control of my weekly gift

only meet me in the water
where I'm granted equal footing
I can walk to you with life, life, life
self propelled limbs feel female

16

as strength surges to support
where outside my water-world
gravity lets me down
only ask me to live with you in water

Lots of houses in Bristol were huge and ours was no exception. There were thirteen rooms and a cellar, where I was often put to have afternoon naps in a pram in amongst the gardening tools and piles of tins and coal. I remember so clearly Mummy's face as she tucked me in, saying 'snug as a bug in a rug'. My bedroom was right at the top in the attic; I would guess that it was once the maid's room. My parents' bedroom was downstairs and my mother's parents had four rooms in between, where they lived independently. I adored Granny, she was wonderful. She regularly gave me Huntley and Palmer's breakfast biscuits with butter on them, and when she gave me raisins she told me to 'bite them up well'. She sang to me every night from an old black hymn book, 'Gentle Jesus, meek and mild' and we would sing together as well, 'Jesus loves me, this I know, for the Bible tells me so'. I still remember, 'Jesus wants me for a sunbeam'. But Granny wasn't all choruses; she would sit and help me learn my tables and taught me all the tricks of the dreaded tables trade. I had to recite them for my teacher, and if I went wrong I had to come back and start again another day. I can picture Grandpa with ultra-white hair and matching beard in a grey suit and leather slippers. I remember him being quite stern. I was a bit scared of him because of his false teeth which he would click in and out, and I used to think they might fall out. But I loved him.

As a brood of children my brothers and I were the usual noisy and energetic types. On Sundays, long before my parents were up, we used to slide down the stairs. There were four flights of stairs in our old Victorian house and our rooms were at the top. We took the mattresses off my brothers' bunk beds, put them on the stairs, put a sheet on top and then slid down. We would all land in a heap at the bottom until our parents woke up and yelled at us to stop because we were making so much noise. We also made houses out of sheets and mattresses, dark and igloo-shaped, and I would suddenly get scared and have to get out but sometimes I was too late and the whole thing collapsed on top of me.

We earned our pocket money by helping clean and tidy around the house and by picking the mulberries off the big mulberry tree in the garden. The berries that we didn't eat went into lots of different pies and puddings. That tree was full of adventure. I had a swing in it which was good for me because of the exercise. My parents were always looking for ways to help me maintain my strength. On my sixth birthday, when I went into hospital, my father bought me a tricycle and put it on a stand so that I could practise pedalling. I was very keen on my new toy and even the doctor saw that I was determined to pedal this tricycle every day because I knew how important it was to get the exercise, even at the age of six.

There were the usual sibling jealousies, of course, that were perhaps more extreme for me because of my small size and disability. I couldn't reach the saucepans and taste the cooking, so I used to be quite the spiteful little horror when Andrew succeeded in doing what I could not manage. There was a lot of, 'Mummy! Andrew's picking the curry. Andrew's stolen some malt.' Andrew, in particular, had a sweet tooth and would take and eat a whole raw jelly and hide the packets under his mattress, as well as packets of biscuits. I once put surgical spirit in a mug of water for Andrew as a 'clever' act of revenge. He informed me angrily that he could go blind because of it and I burst into tears and was racked with guilt for days.

Andrew is two and a half years older and Simon nearly six years older than me. I was four when Alcuin was born at home. When my mother found that she was pregnant with Alcuin she was very upset and didn't want the baby. They knew by then that I had got muscular dystrophy. She felt she could just about cope with one disabled child, but not another baby as well. However, long before the end of the pregnancy she had completely changed. A sense of well-being had come. She really wanted the baby and went round proudly telling people, 'I'm forty and I'm having a baby'. I was really disappointed that he wasn't a girl. I had prayed so hard for a little sister, feeling I had enough brothers already. I really believed I would get a sister. When I didn't, I felt God had really let me down this time. The feeling didn't last, of course.

I was also media conscious even in my youth and chose to write to William Hardcastle on the subject of the physically 'handicapped', as I called myself then, before I came to prefer the adjective 'disabled'.

Dear William Hardcastle,

I am writing to tell you about Physically Handicapped people. For a start I am Physically handicapped I am 9 years old and have Musculardistrophy. I am very thankful I do not have to go about in a Wheelchair. I have injections which daddy gives to me and a special kind of shoe on my left leg. I think people who are handicapped ought not just stay in bed for weeks and weeks and months and months or they will get weaker and won't be able to walk. I think people ought to go outside and get freshair. If there was a fire in a handicapped hospital people shouldn't wait until they are fetched out of the fire but try to help themselves a bit. In other words they ought not to wait for everything to be done for them but try first.

If people go past a model of a child who is handicapped holding a collecting box they sometimes think to themselves oh isn't it sad that some children are handicapped but I won't waste my money on things like that, and they don't think that if they were handicapped they would like people to collect money for them.

I don't go to a school for handicapped children I go to High School. Which is very near us. At school we do

19

gymn, netball and dancing I do gymn and dancing but not netball.

Yours sincerely, Miss E. Wilkie

P.S. If you do put my letter on the Radio Please don't do in the term time (Term starts this coming Thursday).

I never heard it broadcast, though perhaps I was at school.

As I grew older and weaker I became more and more aware of the implications of my disability. My mother recalls one time when she was helping me bath and I asked, 'Mummy, was it because of something you took when you were expecting me that I am like I am?' I was about nine years old then and had been listening to a radio programme where the interviewer was talking to mothers who had taken the thalidomide pill. The mothers said that they felt guilty for taking the drug and this made me think.

My mother replied, 'No, it's nothing I took. I know that God gave you to us as you are.'

'Oh, that's all right, then. I thought you might be feeling guilty.' It is my mother who remembers that conversation, for it touched her that my main concern was not over my disability but that she should not feel guilty.

Whilst my mother and I agreed on many things, the subject of the length of my hair was always a fraught one. It was the Sixties and everyone had long flowing locks. But my mother insisted that this would not suit me so my hair was always cut short, so short in fact that I was often mistaken for a boy. One year when my brothers were actually growing their hair long, my mother had mine done short again, but the hairdresser cut it far shorter than my mother had intended. It was horrible, and cut really badly. I was desperately upset because soon afterwards we went on holiday to France, me wearing my usual jeans and a T-shirt, cast-offs from my

brothers which I did like wearing, and people sometimes thought I was the boy and one of my brothers
the girl. People in shops would say, *'Regarde le petit
garçon,'* and I would growl, *'Pas un petit garçon. Une
petite fille!'*

Holidays were about the only time when my brothers
ever complained about me and my disability, and that
was because I couldn't do the washing up quickly
enough so that they could go down to the beach. If they
ever resented me more than that they never said so and
as far as I know they never complained about my getting
extra attention, which I didn't get anyway. I was disciplined and smacked if I was naughty, just as the boys
were.

By the beginning of the summer we were all eagerly
anticipating 'le camping sauvage' in France, our regular
family holiday. I could walk until I was fourteen or so and
being in tents was very accessible, as was sleeping on the
ground, so we did not need to worry about special
facilities. It was more difficult later on, when we had to
get my pushchair down to the beach, although it was
no worse than pushing a child in a pram. The other
thing that got more difficult as I got weaker was that
I could no longer balance properly over the hole that
we dug for the loo. The first time I fell in, I went up
to my ankle. The second time I went in up to my
knee and then up to my armpits. That was disgust-
ing. I was fished out, washed down and talced. It was
awful, I shall never forget it. After that we took our
own loo.

It was before one such holiday that Grandpa died,
when I was just eight. We were all picking mulberries
that day when my mother came to stand in the doorway,
with tears pouring down her face saying, 'Grandpa's just
died.' I remember travelling to the funeral in a big black
car, feeling very solemn. People cried throughout the
service and there was a huge coffin. I remember standing
by the grave and looking down into the deep black hole. I
met death quite young – it wasn't all hushed up. We all

went along to the funeral, which I think made us accept it a bit more.

Death

death
 is
the final fact
 of
life

2

'In nature there's no blemish but the mind;
None can be call'd deform'd but the unkind'
William Shakespeare

My parents used to be Exclusive Brethren, a sect of
Christians who keep themselves separate from the rest of
the world. They regard their separation from the world as
not only spiritual but also physical, obeying strict regulations. So some of the more extreme members build
churches with high windows to emphasise this separation and to prevent people from seeing in. Daddy's
family remained Exclusive Brethren throughout their
lives.

Because of their exclusive faith we were unable to see
my grandmother all that often. In fact, on our Christmas
visit we children were always told that we did not eat
with Granny Wilkie because we had a meal waiting for us
with our cousins in Leicester, which was true, except that
we did not eat with Granny Wilkie because the Exclusive
Brethren are not allowed to eat with outsiders. When my
grandmother died, there was even a lot of opposition
to my father going to the funeral. I shall never forget
sitting in our kitchen with Great Grandpa's old farmhouse clock-on-the-wall pendulum ticking away the
seconds and my father's choked voice speaking with
distressed firmness to his brother-in-law, 'She's my
mother, Bill, not yours.' Even Aunty Eileen, my father's
sister, stopped sending me birthday presents after a

while, and on our last Christmas visit to them there was no reply to our knock, although we believe they were in the house.

My father's father died when I was very young, when we were still in touch with the rest of the family. He had Parkinson's disease and so his movements were sometimes uncontrolled. I'm told that when I was three, still unaware of my own disability and unabashed by other people's, I used to wave to him, thinking that when his hands were shaking he was actually waving to me. It seems that children often respond in a far less judgmental way to disability, for they have not yet developed any prejudices.

When my parents came out of the Exclusive Brethren they originally met with other ex-Exclusives for a Sunday Service. The meeting room was near Bristol docks, so in the summer I used to walk to the docks afterwards with my brothers to see the swans and the ships. One of my earliest memories is of my younger brother Alcuin's baptism in our bath, when I was four and he was a baby. We all crowded into the bathroom and I was worried that Alcuin would drown when he was submerged. The best bit was having a bath in the same water afterwards because we were never usually allowed it that deep. The water was green and I thought it was as good as being in a swimming pool. We went to a Baptist church later on; I remember my mother holding me up against the pews so that I could sing the hymns standing up.

As a consequence of my Christian background I can't remember a time when I did not know God. I went on a week-long Crusader camp every year from the age of ten until I was about fifteen, and then I moved on to the 'CruFellowship' senior section. Crusaders are a non-denominational organisation devoted to providing Christian teaching for young people.

Every night throughout my early years I asked God to help me get my leg better. I once found a notebook where I wrote, while still quite little: 'Things that worry me: a)

24

swimming b) when I try to get my leg better and things just seem to go wrong.'

After my left foot had started growing crooked I was fitted with a night splint. I wore it for several years. It was quite a vicious thing. It looked like something out of Dickens. It used to rip the sheets to shreds because it had a long prong on it with a loop and a leather strap to pull my foot straight. It was agony. I don't remember going through a night with it on properly, because it stopped me sleeping. I always used to loosen it and then tighten it just before my mother came in, to make it look as though I had worn it tight all night. I wanted to but the pain was too great. That was probably why I associated my disability with my leg and why I prayed for my leg rather than my muscular dystrophy to get better. It was the only tangible evidence that I had a disability at that stage. In actual fact, my shortened foot tendons were a secondary problem caused by the muscle biopsy and had nothing to do with the muscular dystrophy at all.

I made my conscious commitment to Christianity when I was eight. The ex-Exclusive service had no liturgy, it was just like Open Brethren, really, or Quakers, with people speaking or suggesting hymns when they felt 'moved' to. As a result I was strongly against structured church services and felt unhappy with rigid rules. One day I heard that if you had not asked Jesus into your heart, you weren't a Christian and I got terribly worried because I didn't remember having done that. I thought God was already there. So when I got home that night, in bed I said, 'Oh Jesus, if you're not in there, come in quick.' I wondered from time to time whether I was a Christian and how I could be sure. I went to my Crusader camp leader when I was about thirteen to ask for a book which was recommended for those who were not sure of their faith. I asked her sheepishly for the booklet 'How Can I Be Sure I'm a Christian?'

She said, 'Oh, but you are you're sure you are!' and I felt so stupid that I had asked for the book and revealed my uncertainty because *she* was obviously sure of my Christianity.

Partly because my parents had an Exclusive background, our family had no television. They did not agree with the Exclusives that it was an instrument of the Devil, but they thought it probably did more harm than good. They considered it would be better if we developed our imaginations and read, which of course is true and we all became avid readers. But if anything made me feel left out at school it was not my physical disability but the 'disability' of no television. People were always saying, 'Oh, did you see such and such on the telly?' and didn't understand why I didn't watch. I loved telly (probably only because it was 'forbidden fruit') and I used to go across the road to Anne O'Neill's to watch it. I loved going over there because she had things I never had – television, chocolate finger biscuits and comics.

The irony is that now I am on television as a part of my job. I have had a television since living in London, but my parents only recently bought one when they thought they could no longer go round to somebody else's house in order to watch me! They neither of them watch it frequently, nor do they only watch me.

My stage career began when I was five. My acting debut was as an angel, with a halo, a new white dress made specially for me from white sheets and, of course, wings. I had to kneel down all through the play and I wore lipstick, which was wonderful because I really liked the taste of it. I was truly angelic and did nothing but lick my lips and pick my nose throughout.

Later on I played Puck in *A Midsummer Night's Dream* which we did in the school garden holding the books as we acted because we hadn't learned our lines. I was dressed almost all in green with green tights and a green cotton jerkin. I had made some cardboard ears, goblin-like, put them on a piece of elastic and wore them round my head. I must have looked so funny with spindly legs and a wobbly walk, declaiming, 'I'll put a girdle round the Earth in forty minutes.'

I have wanted to be an actress since the age of twelve but when I plucked up courage to tell my mother she said it wasn't possible. I know she had no moral objections but was thinking of my disability. I thought, 'I'm stupid. If I can't walk, I can't walk across a stage.' I suppressed my true self by thinking about jobs like being a museum curator, librarian, or an archivist and I was quite content to follow up those occupations. Later in my teens I joined the Bristol Old Vic Theatre Club and was carried upstairs backstage to join in with the playreading group; it was then that I felt I belonged in the theatre and had an inkling I'd work in that field one day.

Meanwhile, my school acting career continued and I gave it all I'd got. In the house play competition I played a nurse. This was not a speaking part and I was disappointed at that. Most of the time I had to sit behind a curtain and during one scene the curtain was opened and I had to mop the fevered brow of the sick father, played by a friend of mine. I had a white cloth and white basin. Unfortunately the cloth dried out and went stiff and scratchy, so I had to try not to scratch my friend's forehead while putting everything into the part and using all my talent to show what a wonderful actress I was.

Although my disability worsened throughout my childhood, at no time did I go to a special school for disabled children. I started off at the local primary school, although the boys there teased me a bit. I thought they were taking advantage of me and looking up my skirt. Maybe they were but I don't suppose they teased me any more than any of the other girls! In any case, I transferred to a direct-grant all girls' school. The pupils there accepted me straight away as one of them; perhaps it was easier then because I was still walking and didn't have to be pushed around in a wheelchair. However, no one's attitude changed when I was no longer able to walk. My friends were great and helped to make my schooldays full of mostly happy memories. They never complained even when they had to lug me around the school,

27

although staff attitudes were more varied and became more troublesome in later years.

I say 'varied' because at one time I had a form mistress who seemed to delight in making life difficult for me, trying to organise me. She even prevented me going off with the rest of the school to see an exhibition in London because she said if there was a bomb they wouldn't be able to get me out in time, whereas, the previous year another teacher had gone out of her way to make special arrangements for me on a similar outing. I remember I once commented to this teacher that I quite liked the idea of being a school librarian. I was smartly informed that it would be impossible for me because I wouldn't be able to reach the top shelf.

In my early years of schooling my headmistress at the junior school had a very different attitude. Since I had to be carried up and down stairs she made it fun for me. There were three ways of carrying me: the 'porpoise', being carried sideways so I was sort of swimming upstairs; 'sack of potatoes', which was over her shoulder, and – the most daring and dangerous – the 'elephant', my favourite one. This meant she picked me up with my back to her front and held me under my knees so my legs waved like a trunk.

I had all the normal likes and dislikes of any school child. I was lousy at maths and I hated sport so it was just as well that I had to miss it. While my classmates were out on the freezing hockey field I was set to practising my handwriting which was appalling. It was improving dramatically until the weekend I did a project on silkworms. Of course they all hatched out at the same time! I remember frantically recording each hatching, distracted from all thoughts about my handwriting. It was so exciting to see the whole thing happening in front of my eyes. Not only did I write about each hatching but I also drew them, so it was all very messy. I handed in my report and thought nothing more about it. I believe it got lost internally, until one day my teacher began talking about someone's project. At first I didn't take any notice of what she was saying. She was waving something about and I didn't think it had anything to do with me, but then she described the project and said it was very good but the handwriting was dreadful. I realised then that it was mine. The teacher must have found it somewhere. I was now in a dilemma; obviously I wanted to take credit for the good project, but I was embarrassed that the whole class now knew the teacher's opinion of my handwriting. Eventually I plucked up courage to say in a non-committal way, 'Oh, I think it might be mine.'

I have always expressed emotions of sadness, hurt or frustration through tears. When I was eight my form mistress wrote on my report under the heading 'Social Response': 'Apart from the short period when she was easily upset and rather tearful, Ellen has had a happy term.' I was a highly sensitive child, but I think crying is far more healthy than bottling up emotions which will eventually manifest themselves in more ugly ways. It is a shame it is so un-English to cry in public; sensitivity has its positive side, too, in human relationships.

Apart from being sensitive, I was always very healthy and could never manage to be ill enough to have a day off school. I did once try putting a thermometer in a cup of tea to give myself a falsely high temperature, but this resulted in the threat of bed without supper so I had to confess: I was too hungry to hold out.

It was not until I reached the Sixth Form that the storm broke and I was forced to face up to other people's attitudes to my disability, especially in the adult world. The drama that unfolded at school came as a total shock.

Quite suddenly the school announced that they wanted me to go to a special college for the 'handicapped' after I'd finished my 'O' Levels, so that I could 'learn to cope with my disability'. My parents were called to a meeting with the headmistress at which they were told that it would be in my 'best interests' to leave my school and go to a college for the 'physically handicapped'. The headmistress gave my parents two brochures about such institutions. My father pointed out that my best chance in the future was to get good 'A' Level results, and if I needed special training I could get that later. The discussion continued throughout that 'O' Level year. I wasn't told anything because they didn't want to upset me. My parents had always encouraged me to live as normal a life as possible. Eventually, though, I found out. It was obvious that something was going on with all those letters and meetings. I asked them what it was that they were hiding from me. So they told me and I was very angry.

I felt that special schools did not help disabled people manage in the real world, nor help people without disability to relate to the disabled. Often, their academic standards and opportunities were not as high as in an ordinary school. I would not be able to do the 'A' Levels I planned to do, nor would I necessarily be able to achieve the high standard I had attained so far (I had seven 'O' Levels) because my attention would be divided between learning academically and learning to 'cope' with my disability. Apart from a very limited range of academic subjects, the only courses offered were things like book-keeping and typewriting. Besides, I had been integrated into the outside world throughout my life. Where was the advantage in going to a special school? But my parents had to fight tooth and nail to keep me where I was. The whole process was lengthy and very painful.

My parents got advice from the headmistress of the junior school, who had always bent over backwards to help me. It was her decision to accept me into the school in the first place. She told my parents to ask for my timetable for the new term, so that it would give us time to plan my movements. One of the school's objections was that I sometimes needed help getting up and down flights of stairs between classrooms, or along the corridors. It had never been a problem for some of the other pupils to carry me. I only weighed about three stone then and have always been very small. I think I would have been petite anyway because my mother only weighs six stone. I could manage by myself in the classrooms but now the school was saying the other pupils should not carry me. With a timetable, we might at least be able to see what, if any, tricky distances might be involved, and make the necessary arrangements. The timetable was normally not drawn up until late in the academic year. However, the school never sent the timetable – so what were my parents supposed to do?

My father asked if they would be given a term's notice before the school expelled me, and they reassured him that they would do so. We never got that notice, so of course I turned up for the first day of my 'A' Level course. That was when the real trouble began. The teachers said, 'What are you doing here? You shouldn't be here – you should have made other arrangements.' But what other arrangements could we have made when we had heard nothing from the school governors?

My brother, Andrew, and my oldest brother's fiancée had brought me up to school that day. For the first time, I was not in uniform. I was wearing a gold corduroy trouser suit that I'd made myself, my favourite outfit, with orange hippy love beads round my neck, and a brown cotton jersey shirt with a big collar and a jazzy pattern. It was very Seventies. I was looking forward to starting work and concentrating on the subjects that I really enjoyed. But before I had even set foot in the building, I was told by a teacher to go to the front hall instead of my form room. The front hall was basically a waiting area outside the head's room where you could sit and look at a collection of boring free magazines that nobody wanted to read. It was very humiliating for me to sit there with people walking past the whole time.

I was upset and I cried. My future sister-in-law was sitting next to me, looking like a typical farmer's daughter in brown cords and an anorak, with a pair of dirty socks in her pockets. The headmistress swept out of her room, caught sight of her and demanded, 'And who on earth are *you*?'

'Well, I'm Ellen's brother's fiancée, actually.'

It had been raining that morning and the headmistress's umbrella was standing in the hall and Andrew, hanging around to see what would happen to me, picked it up.

'What shall I do with this?' he said. 'Hang it from the chandelier?' trying to make light of the situation and have a bit of a joke.

Right on cue, the headmistress again came out of the study and Andrew whipped the umbrella behind his back.

'Young man, young man!' she thundered. 'Give that to me!'

'Oh, terribly sorry,' said Andrew. 'Here, please have it back. I had no idea it was yours.' It was a lighter moment, but it didn't last.

My school friends came along to see if there was anything they could do. They wanted to go in and talk to the head to say that they didn't mind carrying me, but in the end they decided this would do more harm than good, as nobody would listen.

I was not allowed to go to my classroom, and had to stay on that chair outside the headmistress's room. My brother Andrew was very upset and went to my form mistress to give her my dinner cheque. I had actually been given a teacher and a form room even though I wasn't supposed to be in the school. It all seemed like a plot against me. Even my form mistress refused to take the dinner cheque, although she was new to the school and knew nothing about me! She walked past me as I was sitting in the front hall and was obviously dying to know who this rebel was. None of the other teachers would look at me but she gave me a quick sidelong stare as she went past.

Andrew then went to the school secretary but even she said she couldn't possibly accept my cheque. My mother was phoned and the head asked her to take me home, but we knew that once we gave way, that would be it. My mother would have taken me away if I'd wanted, but I said I wasn't moving. The headmistress was saying things like, 'This is my school and I make the rules,' and I replied, 'Well, it's my school, too!'

When it came to lunchtime I was not allowed to sit in the dining room. The headmistress came out to me and said very patronisingly, 'Would you like me to bring you your lunch here?' It was a revolting meal – steak and kidney pie, which I can't stand anyway, hard carrots and boiled potatoes, covered with cold gravy and followed by sponge pudding and custard – and she brought it to me as if it were a banquet on a silver platter.

By the afternoon we'd come to some sort of a compromise whereby my mother was allowed to come in and take me up to the Sixth Form house where my lessons were. I just wanted to bite the headmistress when she patted me on the head. She asked me to promise 'not to let anybody touch you'. Only my mother was allowed to take me round the school, as a temporary agreement. The school was sticking to its argument that none of the other girls could be expected to carry me. Nothing started until the afternoon anyway because of the usual beginning of term arrangements, giving out timetables and checking gym kits, so I hadn't missed any lessons. For the rest of the week, my mother was told she had to come and take me from lesson to lesson.

When I did get my timetable it turned out that all my lessons were in the same building, so the help I would need would be minimal.

The second day was my busiest day, with seven lessons, compared to every other day when I only had two or three. I wasn't going to miss it but the school were surprised when I turned up accompanied by my mother. A special meeting of the governors was arranged for the next day, a Saturday, to tackle my 'case'. My parents attended.

At the meeting, one of the governors, a paediatrician, said firmly that every person with muscular dystrophy should be in an institution and that integration was a very bad idea. She had never met me so was not really in a position to judge, but this was what we were up against.

My father vividly remembers how everyone then went round the school to discover how much walking about was included in 'a typical sixth former's day'. None of it was actually relevant to my 'typical day', so the exercise was very misleading. No one looked at my timetable. They began with Morning Prayers, which is not obligatory, then counted the steps down to the Lower Sixth Form room in the basement even though I didn't really need to go there. They even counted all the steps to the chemistry labs, although I wasn't studying the subject, I was doing Latin, Greek and French. The triumphant announcement was, 'There are 132 steps in a typical sixth former's day, therefore . . .' In fact, all my lessons were on one floor, which I could still manage to get around unaided. I could even manage the stairs up to the Sixth Form common room, above the classrooms.

My parents asked if there had been any complaints from other girls' parents about carrying me at school, but they admitted there hadn't been any. Of course, when all the fuss started, some did worry that the lifting might cause gynaecological problems, but when a gynaecologist was consulted he said, rather than any risk of damage, the exertion would do them good!

The whole thing was like an infection that spread, and all those teachers whom I thought were happy with my presence suddenly had doubts. I felt betrayed. My French teacher, for example, a young woman who had been friendly towards me, joined the 'wets' and toed the party line. She had been very happy for me to do 'A' Level before the crisis, and then she came up to me, blushing bright red, and said, 'But, Ellen, how would you cope with the literature?'

My English teacher had also made this comment when I had considered English 'A' Level. She said I would be reading about things in literature that I could not possibly be able to experience and it would be very upsetting for me. I believe she underestimated me (perhaps she thought I could not have a sex life), and in any case everybody reads about things they never experience, that is part of the reason for reading.

One of my classics teachers, however, was more supportive, and really wanted me to stay in the school. She seemed to be aware of the sort of conspiracy that was going on. Unfortunately, she was in her first term as vice-head, which put her in a difficult position and limited her ability to help.

In the middle of all this chaos, the Chairman of the Governors actually chased my mother, ran after her through the school. It was like a scene from a farce. 'Mrs Wilkie! Mrs Wilkie! Come back!' He wanted to talk to her but she refused to do so without my father being there. Even as she ran out of the school, the school secretary barred her way at the door. My mother just glared at her and she stepped aside. My mother ran all the way home and burst into tears in my father's arms when she got there.

After the Governors' meeting I went to an independent paediatrician for my physical condition to be assessed, as my parents thought this would add weight to our cause. A paediatrician seemed rather inappropriate anyway because by now I was sixteen, more adult than child. When we arrived at his surgery it was like a nursery with toys all over the place. The doctor had an unpleasant manner and was very aggressive. He made me walk upright, which I could only manage with my mum helping me, so he shouted at me, 'You're not doing it! Do it yourself!' And when I went alone, crouching near the ground, he shouted, 'That's not walking, do it properly!' When I failed to do it properly, he said with satisfaction, 'See, you can't do it!'

Then I had to go to a freezing cold room, take all my clothes off except for my knickers and sit and wait for ages. I could hear him talking and shouting at my mother in the next room. Then he came in and started examining me. He did a full examination. I was furious, I felt like a piece of meat. He started talking about my problems.

'I haven't really got any problems,' I said.

35

'Oh yes you have,' he replied. 'There it is, it's you. A big problem.'

When I was back with my mother I just burst into tears and I said I was never, ever going back there again. The doctor treated me like a small child who thought she knew what was best for her, but was too stupid to understand the situation. In the end, the school did not want this report, so all the hassle had been a waste of time.

After that Saturday meeting with school officials my parents had to provide a rota of people from outside the school to help me round during the day, each one reporting to the headmistress on arrival. My mother remembers being greeted with a cold cup of tea and a stale biscuit. One of the people who joined the rota was a parent who helped organise a petition to the Board of Governors. The letters she wrote made all the points that we had been making and said that with a 'little humanity and flexibility on the part of the school' my remaining two years could be made far easier. She asked that the 'absurd requirement' that I have a constant attendant should be dropped. She gave numerous and well-thought-out reasons why I should stay and made many simple practical suggestions about how my stay could be made easier; for instance, not going to Morning Prayers which was a right of any pupil anyway. She pointed out that most of my friends were almost of the age to be nurses, when they would have to lift weights much heavier than my three stone. Her reasoning was sound and there was not really any cogent argument against her. The only argument there could be, and which the school stuck to as long as it could, was that disabled people should not be integrated. This view was only really held by one paediatrician on the Board of Governors who influenced the headmistress.

The petition to allow me to be kept in school, which 251 parents signed, in the end worked. One parent rang up someone on the school council to find out about the situation. They were told by this councillor that he just could not care less what happened to me. This incited righteous indignation which fuelled the fight to keep me there.

Although the idea of integrating disabled children into mainstream schools was still relatively new, and I was unusual in being at my school, I didn't feel unusual in myself. It was the attitudes of the other people that were handicapping me; it was nothing to do with what I could or could not manage with my disability. I have never thought, 'Oh no, my legs are so weak, I can't walk,' and that's nothing to do with being brave. I just feel like me, sitting in a chair, and I don't think about how I move around as very different from most people. When I looked up the word 'handicapped' in a dictionary, I found it meant 'something imposed on you which hampers', and that's exactly what I discovered – that other people were imposing, and have imposed at various times in my life, their own handicapping prejudices on me, putting me down into a disadvantaged position. It is this attitude, more than narrow doorways and split-level corridors, which makes life difficult for disabled people. For the first time in my life, I was made to feel that having muscular dystrophy would prevent me from having a normal life, if other people got their way.

The headmistress said all along to my parents, 'Of course it's all in Ellen's best interests,' but I was never consulted. Most of the governors had never met me. They had conducted their entire discussion without me. That is typical of the attitude that says, 'Disabled people don't know what's best for them.'

Up until then my disability had not really been an issue because I hadn't felt any different from other people. I'd always carried on doing the same things that my brothers had done: I hadn't really had to think about it. It was a dreadful shock to find my disability stopping me from doing something that I knew I could do. However, it wasn't really my disability but other people's attitudes that were frustrating me and that is almost worse.

It was ridiculous to be told that I ought to 'learn to cope

with my handicap' because that's something you learn throughout your life. You don't 'learn to cope with a disability', you learn to cope with life with a disability. It's more demanding, maybe, for someone who is disabled but that is all part of the process. There are no lessons on the curriculum which teach you to cope with life at school. Things like managing money, managing relationships, doing your own laundry, budgeting income, those things are not taught at school. In just the same way, you don't go to classes where the teacher says, 'Now, everyone, today you are going to learn to cope with your disability.' What I now had to learn to cope with was other people's attitudes, that's what was handicapping me. If only they could have realised the irony of what they were saying. It was they who had to learn to cope with my disability.

When it looked as though I was going to be staying at the school after all, my friends suddenly had to have written permission from their parents to help carry me when necessary. But the school had always been keen on red tape. They made you get written permission for every possible situation, from going on a trip to wearing your indoor shoes outdoors. I recall writing to my best friend and frequent correspondent, Rosie: 'On July 8th we are going on a sixth form picnic. I was told that Miss H. has given me permission to go. What downright cheek. Isn't it pathetic? I have to have *permission* to go on a sixth form picnic. I can't stand school at the moment. I wish it was this time next year, then I would be doing "A" Levels and would soon be leaving.'

Once having received this permission to carry me, the girls had to choose a, b, c, or d ways of helping. It was made completely objective. They were grown women by now, but the school seized on this as another 'difficulty'.

I found the whole thing totally humiliating, and when I was being carried round the school, I felt as though all eyes were upon me. I had never felt like that before. Throughout my 'O' Level year, although I knew something was going to happen, I had no idea it would be this, although I do pride myself on being quite an intuitive person. At the end of my 'O' Level year I'd wondered what was going on, with all these letters being exchanged, but my friends all said, 'Oh, it'll be fine. Don't worry, of course you'll be coming back in September.' Even so, sometimes deep inside me something told me that things were more serious than they seemed. I tried to ignore this feeling and get on with enjoying the summer holidays. Now I've learnt to listen to my intuitive feelings because they're invariably right. Sometimes I did think, 'I just want to get right away from this,' but that was just escapism: I stuck it out.

At the end of it all, we had to fight the press off. I wanted to be in the papers, but it wouldn't have helped matters because the situation had been settled (fairly) amicably. The school agreed 'ungrudgingly to accept her back'. They had to put it like that, even though I'd not officially left.

When I look back on it now, it seems to have happened to someone else. I can't believe it all happened to me. It's too extraordinary – petitions from parents and governors' meetings. We were carried along through the different events, as if in a dreamworld, from one day to the next, eating and sleeping and trying to sort it all out. All through this time there was an awareness of a supernatural presence being the carrier behind the chaos, and I believe we did find refuge in the shadow of those immense wings.

In the end, the headmistress didn't have any choice. On the day of the final council meeting in the library, I was at the school. Whenever there was a meeting there would always be notices on blackboards at the bottom of the stairs: 'Quiet – meeting in progress'. This time, as I went past the library, I knew exactly what they were talking about. They voted unanimously for me to stay.

3

*'My life is changing in so many ways I don't know
who to trust any more. I shall be going through
my days like a beggar who goes from door to door'*
Neil Young

'There are only three things in life worth worrying about:
your health, personal relationships and, of course, the
Almighty.' This conversation was a big turning point in
my life. I had gone to my personal tutor, Jim Tester, in
tears. It was the middle of my second year at university
and I had what students call 'second-year blues'. I was
behind in my assessed essays which contributed to my
degree, and I had post-flu depression, so I told him, 'I
can't cope with this, it's all too much but I don't want to
be a failure.' In his warm and cosy academic room he
handed me a comforting tissue and spoke words of
reassurance. His reply put everything into perspective
and he certainly lived by what he said. He sometimes
cancelled seminars because he had taken the dog for a
walk or gone to the dentist, and if students missed
seminars, instead of reprimanding them he would say,
'It's your choice,' whereas other lecturers were less sym-
pathetic and sent notes to students demanding an explanation of their absence. Sadly, he died of cancer a few
years ago, but his effect on me has been lasting. From
then on, although I never stopped worrying completely,
I did begin to get things into proportion. Whenever I felt
ugly little worries creeping in I deliberately recalled Jim

Tester's pearls of wisdom. Life's too short to do otherwise.

I had applied to do Classics at Bristol University because it was only a stone's throw (if you are good at throwing stones) from where I lived. My interview to get on to the course had been very tough. I had two interviewers, one 'old school' type who bombarded me with a barrage of awkward questions, such as comparing some literary aspect of Jane Austen with Sophocles' *Oedipus the King*, and a quiet, sweet interviewer who at this unbearable point butted in and lifted me out of very deep water by saying 'I'd find that question difficult to answer myself.' I went home despondent, convinced that I was going to be rejected, so I was amazed when they said they would accept me with two E grades at 'A' level. In fact, despite finding exams difficult throughout my school career, I got one A and two Bs plus an 'S' level, so studying at Bristol was never really in doubt.

My mother went to see the tutor for admissions to find out how the university would suit (or otherwise) a student in a wheelchair. By now I had been forced to succumb to what I'd so far managed to steer well clear of – the dreaded wheelchair. I was quite rightly convinced that as soon as I 'took to' (or was dragged to) an indoor wheelchair-image I'd be treated as a lesser being. As long as I could get along under my own steam, however inelegantly, I felt an equal in everyone's eyes. The institutional blue D.H.S.S. wheelchair was a practical necessity to get from A to B in the institution of learning where I was to embark on my three years of academic life. Well, I could hardly get around on my haunches along the vast corridors of a mock-Gothic Victorian building, could I?

I had all my lectures in this building. It had a massive flight of steps leading up to it but, luckily for me, there was a side door which had only one step, so the university provided a movable wooden ramp. Ironically and annoyingly, it was not until I had left Bristol that the ramp was concreted in. I noticed it during the International Year of Disabled People. It was a shame somebody

41

had to wait that long to do what they could have done for me because all through my course I had to rely on a fellow-student to meet me and put the ramp down. As a result I sometimes arrived at my nine o'clock lectures half an hour late. I would be stranded outside the building thinking, 'I don't believe it! Why is this happening to me again?' but help always did arrive, with apologies for the delay, frequently bleary-eyed, staggering and dragging on a cigarette.

At this time in my life I was going through a sort of transition period with regard to my disability. I'd begun to use the indoor wheelchair in my student environment, even though I still used my own muscle power to get around on the level and to 'bum' it up and down stairs at home. With the money I saved from my monthly mobility allowance I had purchased a smart new outdoor wheelchair, 'Electra', in the Upper Sixth. It was a 'battery-powered three-wheeler pavement vehicle' which looked something like a cross between a lawn-mower and a chair, so it did not stigmatise me instantly. At last I was 'free' and could go where I liked – or so I thought. In fact it was not quite as easy as that, as indicated by my dependence on the ramp and the student to put it there. I soon found that my new-found freedom was somewhat restricted. I became embarrassed at continually being stuck in shop doorways or scratching the paintwork, and frustrated at reaching a shop only to find that there were steps to prevent my going in.

Electra did have its advantages though. I was shopping one day in Broadmead when a man tried to flog me some decidedly dubious literature. He was very insistent but I was equally keen on making a quick get-away and, in my speedy attempt, I accidentally ran over his foot. He was so surprised, and the whole situation was so funny, that I burst out laughing while apologising, so of course he thought I'd done it on purpose.

On reflection I'm amazed at my daring and complete lack of fear in Electra. I treated the vehicle like a motor-bike, which was not difficult because it gathered momentum going downhill and far exceeded its legal limit of four miles per hour. With absolute abandon I allowed myself to become exhilarated by zooming crazily down the middle of the (quieter) local streets, and I'll never forget gleefully 'running' away from my mother after an argument. It was as if my years of being deprived of the ability to move fast under my own steam were being compensated for. I would even go out in the pouring rain, floods and snow. I adopted a pioneering spirit rather than give in and become dependent again. I can recall only one or two times in the whole of my three years of study when, through atrocious weather, I was forced to get a lift from my mother.

Electra made getting to university much easier. Many times I made the journey with Alcuin, who was on his way to school while I was on my way to every student's delight – that nine o'clock lecture. Alcuin was quite useful in fact, especially in the rush hour. He used to yell things like, 'Don't cross now, you stupid cripple, do you want to get run over?' as I was about to launch myself into the path of a passing car. Electra, however, was solely an outdoor vehicle which meant that I had to change wheelchairs when I got to my department. There seemed to be no other disabled people at Bristol, so facilities were limited. For example, all of my tutorials were at the end of split-level corridors. The only way to get round this was to grab an extra-hunky student (any excuse) to lift the bottom end of the chair. There had been a disabled professor at Bristol whose room was still available and I was lent the key to it so that I could use it to change wheelchairs, and later I took my first-year exams there. Mind you, with the common room outside and being on my own inside, it was difficult for me to get my adrenalin going for that exam atmosphere. All my school exams had been taken with my schoolmates. The only concession to me had been that I was allowed a little extra time to compensate for my slowness in writing.

It was also crucial for me not to get stuck high up in the Wills Building, that tall Victorian tower at the top of Park

Street in Bristol, after six o'clock at night when they shut the lifts down. Once or twice I had to be carried down several flights of vast stone stairs, chair and all. Still, with one student at the front and one at the back, I could pretend I was some important person like the Pope.

Books sometimes posed a problem. It was physically difficult for me to get access to all the ones I needed. Actually, the book lists were so shockingly long that you could not possibly read all of them, even if you were the Brain of Britain. However, getting hold of books, I'm ashamed to say, was not a number one priority during my first year.

The amount of work I did for my 'A' Levels probably accounted for how little work I did in my first year at university. Despite Bristol's offer of two Es at 'A' Level, I had not allowed myself to be lulled into a false sense of security. I was ultra-conscientious Ellen, and I still really wanted to do well even though my entrance to university did not depend on it. As a result, I worked very hard in the Sixth Form even though school was never quite the same again after the arguments about my staying on. The whole affair had left a bad taste in my mouth. My courses had been a lot of grinding toil, sweat and labour – sometimes literally. I would spread myself out on the floor in front of the gas fire with my papers scattered in a circle around me, and sometimes fall asleep on a Sunday afternoon over learned tomes on Roman architecture or Greek vase painting. Remember Exekias? Ah, I could hardly forget him, even thirteen years after it was drummed into me that he was the *crème de la crème* of Greek vase painting.

So when I came to Bristol I felt I deserved a rest. I'd been told by Classics students at my interview that the first year was a doss. This was not the case, so one green Wilkie was in for a shock at the vast gap between 'A' Level and first-year undergraduate standard. Even so, I still went wild for a bit, and made sure I enjoyed myself. I did the costumes for the Classical Society's play *Alcestis* in my first year. There were only three of us working on the

44

Wardrobe and we had sixty pounds for all the costumes which included clothing the Greek chorus in long flowing robes. We begged and scrounged old sheets to eke out the meagre budget. Jess Bailey, who has since been with Spandau Ballet, and Alison Moyet composed and played the music. His contribution was the most professional aspect of the production. My career in costume design hasn't gone quite so far.

Neither did my career in archaeology for that matter, judging from a letter I wrote to a friend after two weeks on a university dig: 'I found it great fun washing bits of pottery, bones, nails, mortoria, etc., but even greater fun going to sleep in the sun and having tea breaks!'

As for my proper studies that year, in that same letter I wrote: 'My exams were a failure but that was only to be expected because I didn't take them very seriously (unlike me). The only thing that made me worry about them was that other people were taking them seriously. I've really been taking this year off because I will have to slog next year and the year after to try for a reasonable degree and I would have gone round the bend working hard this year after working solidly for "A" Levels.'

I had imagined I would read Classics in congenial company, but I was to be disillusioned by the Classics students themselves. I hadn't expected them to be boring! I had thought that Classics was a superior subject and attracted a superior *clientèle*. One student really did look like a tramp. He had lurid lime green trousers which he wore tied up with string, flies undone, plus a long woollen red, black and white striped scarf that he wore all the year round, and the obligatory long straggly hair. His staring eyes gazed at you through black-rimmed glasses. He used always to sit right in the middle of the very front row and talk back to the lecturers and ask questions. I felt a bit sorry for him really because the lecturers just spouted. They didn't expect to be asked questions throughout their lectures, and most of them just carried on reading their papers. Our poor philosophy lecturer got the worst of it when one day this student stuck his hand up and asked, 'Was Socrates really a septic?' He looked around to see if we were laughing. We found it hard not to laugh at him, but we did not want to encourage him.

That student was probably the most extreme opposite to my idea of what a Classics student ought to be like. I didn't really mind being in a ragbag of scruffs because I was fairly scruffy myself. But even so, the rest were either interested in football and pubs or were swots, and were hardly the sophisticated, fascinating crowd I had hoped for. Maybe this has as much to say about my own preconceived ideas and tendency to snobbery as it does about the students. Fortunately, a university environment can broaden one's outlook and iron out the wrinkles of prejudice and, despite my initial attitude towards the students, I did not regret doing the subject itself.

On our first day we Classics students were given the customary welcome speech by our Head of Department, Professor Rudd. Any doubts about studying a dead language from a dead culture were dispelled. If people were going to start saying it was pointless to study aspects of the past then, Professor Rudd explained, what was the point of doing Shakespeare, English literature, or even discussing what happened last year? We learn from the past, that's why we study it. His talk really impressed me. As for actually studying the subject, I soon discovered that I had to give up lunchtime drinking; I found I fell asleep in lectures. I kept putting my hands over my eyes in the hope that nobody would notice they were closed, and if I wasn't asleep I wasn't necessarily taking notes either. I frequently wrote letters, like this one to Rosie: 'You just about hit the nail on the head about finding it more difficult to make friends if you were living at home rather than on campus. I didn't realise at first what a drawback it would be, but it was for the first couple of weeks. However, now I have got quite a few friends though not particularly one person with whom I am more friendly than anyone else . . . At the moment

I'm in an extremely boring Roman History lecture and it isn't worth taking notes because the lecturer muddles facts with waffle so as usual I am writing letters. If I haven't got any letters to write, I don't go!'

As I noted in that letter, I definitely felt left out of the real student experience because I was living at home, but that feeling dwindled throughout the course. It was difficult, particularly in the first year, because I didn't get to see people after lectures or seminars. They all lived in hall and had hall discos and shared coffee and so on, while I just went home to the same old way of life.

But I had begun to feel left out earlier than that. Living at home merely highlighted some of the things I had already noticed. In the Sixth Form I had started being aware of my envy of other people doing things I could not do. Suddenly, for the first time in my life, I felt an outsider. It hit me so hard because I was at an age when one becomes increasingly independent – but I was becoming increasingly dependent. I felt the gap was doubly wide. I felt as though my friends were becoming more adult while I was becoming more of a child. This was of course only true in the physical sense. But I felt I had no private life, nothing of my own that wasn't invaded by physical reliance on other people, and so I kept my emotions to myself because they were all I had left to preserve a sense of dignity. Small wonder my mother remarked one day, 'You're so self-contained, Ellen!' Actually, my emotions were poured out into seventeen-page letters to my closest friends, who didn't live anywhere near me. Now an older and wiser woman, I realise becoming 'grown up' has nothing to do with going to pubs and discos, and everything to do with coming to terms with your body letting you down. But at the time, all I could see were people my age being real ravers, doing their homework between lessons and going out in the evenings. They talked about going to pop concerts, discos and pubs with boyfriends and many of them were learning to drive. I couldn't do any of those things spontaneously or on my own. I was still so dependent on my parents that I could not even be a proper teenage rebel. How can you do or say exactly what you feel when you can't make a grand exit by rushing up to your room and slamming the door, and you still need your parents to carry your satchel upstairs or get you out of the bath? Even after my teens, in 1980, I was still writing letters expressing this dissatisfaction: 'I'm going on holiday with my family to France. It won't be much of a holiday if I can't get away from my parents. There's nothing wrong with them, it's just that I hate *having* to go away with them, depend on them, live with them all the time.'

My mother recalls vividly that I came to her one day in floods of tears because I really wanted to take friends out but could never offer to do so because any evening out always entailed lifting me in and out of a car, pushing me and so on. It was no different from *them* taking *me* out and at that stage I was so lacking in self-assertion that I didn't think it right to ask someone out if it meant asking them to do so much for me. I just could not be spontaneous like my other friends could. Sometimes I would see my reflection in the mirror and think 'Why? Why? Why? Why me? Why did God make my body like this?' I began to think a bit more about how rare my particular disability was, how it affected me and none of my brothers. I had a strong feeling that, because it was such a totally freak occurrence, it was as if God were saying to me, 'Look, there's a purpose in all this, I've allowed it to happen to you for a special reason.' It is a hard thing to explain because it is such a personal experience. In bleak times I saw no special reason for it, but deep down inside I did come to feel there was a purpose and it helped, especially when, years later, complete strangers confronted me with things like, 'You know you can be healed.'

I longed to tell people that what was most important about me was not what was wrong with me, or how I had coped with it, but that, inside, my feelings were exactly like everyone else's. I might look different on the outside but I still had the same emotions and traumas as any other girl of nineteen. I had fallen in love at sixteen and, even though my love was unrequited, I still had his letters. I usually made the effort to look cheerful. I felt that, if people could see on my face the agonies I sometimes felt inside, they would treat me differently instead of as one of them, although they did not always do that.

Before I had Electra I had a pushchair, which I used for out of doors and which avoided the wheelchair image but sometimes reinforced the little girl (or little boy!) image. I remember once trying to get in to see some ruins and being informed that the 'No Wheelchairs' rule would not be changed, 'even for the little boy in the pushchair'. In the end they agreed a reduced rate if I would leave the buggy outside and be carried to a bench from where I could sit and look at the ruined abbey. Likewise, at parties, I would be taken out of the buggy and placed on a sofa or on a chair from which I could see what was going on. I was stuck where I was and had to wait for friends to come and say hello, and occasionally they didn't.

Being a great success at a party was, however, sometimes just as awkward as being ignored. My university days, in fashion terms, were the days of baggy shirts and long skirts. I would sit on the sofa in long flowing garb and look very relaxed and 'normal' – so much so that one guy insisted that I should dance with him. I warded off his advances with phrases like, 'No, no, I can't be bothered,' 'I'm too tired' or 'I'm too drunk'. In the end I ran out of excuses but enjoyed the fact that he didn't know I could not walk, let alone dance. Years later, a close friend of mine, Cherif, who had met me at a party under similar circumstances, told me that when he first met me he had thought I was a 'boring cow' who wouldn't dance at parties.

In between socialising and working all hours of the day and night (sometimes all through the night to get an essay in on time) I began to cast some thought to careers. I had begun to realise that life after university does exist, after all. Ever since a conversation about acting with my mother, when I was twelve, I had not considered it a serious option. However, I had no inclination to teach, so

I investigated further the possibility of being an archivist, but soon discovered that it meant doing another academic course. I'd already had enough of academia and had vowed that I would never do another course in my life. Whilst I enjoyed university and have no regrets, by the third year I had had enough. I'd sit in lectures thinking, 'Out there in the real world there are people dying and starving and what am I doing to help them?' The lecturer just went on getting more and more excited about how many meanings he could get out of one sentence in one book by one author in one language. It was obsessive and seemed like insanity. I wanted to get off the academic treadmill.

Thus, by the end of the second year, I had already climbed on to another treadmill, the media treadmill, which involved endless letter writing, frequent rejections and occasional progress. Since I definitely wanted to act and I did not see how I could do it on stage, I decided to try for the next best thing – radio drama. I began to rack my brains for ways of getting a foot, or a wheel, in the door. The first break I had was via a friend of my mother who helped me get the opportunity to give five short talks about myself on B.B.C. Radio Bristol. They were autobiographical accounts of my life and what it was like to be disabled. I wasn't paid and I didn't want to talk about me and disability, but beggars can't be choosers and I was glad of the experience.

Now I had had my first taste of broadcasting I began the letter writing. I wrote to *Morning Story*, the Head of Radio Drama, *Book at Bedtime* and other Radio 4 programmes. The replies told me I could not get work in Drama as yet because I did not have an Equity card. This presented me with some difficulties, as it does all actors, but I was pleased to get a reply at all from these people. Then somebody else suggested I write to *Does He Take Sugar?* I did so although I was a bit reluctant because it was ghetto broadcasting, and I did not want to limit my career by discussing only those issues connected with disability. I did not want to be categorised or put in a box.

they want
to put her in the box
                of their background
to wrap her in the trappings
                of their experience
to tie her with the string
                of their understanding
to stick on her the label
                of their limitations
but they cannot trap
the elusive unknown
in their wrappings
they only dig their own trap
shutting themselves in a box
too dark to see
her unique poetry
too enclosed to hear
her unusual rhythm
and irregular metre
form and content fused
in one breath

the more they pour water
on the burning light
the stronger the flame
consuming night

Does He Take Sugar? wrote back to say that they were
going to do a programme on drama for disabled people,
so would I come along and be interviewed about my
'aspirations'? I was over the moon. Not only had I broken
into the world of Radio 4 (albeit the ghetto slot), but I was
being paid a fee as well! Furthermore, while I was there, I
met someone who told me about a producer who was
putting on a play using professional disabled actors.
They suggested I write to him. Although there was a
four-month delay between my sending the letter and his

receiving it, so that I missed the audition, I did get the opportunity to do some voice-overs offstage. However, the whole episode was pretty unprofessional. I arrived in London, had a script shoved in my hands and was told to do three different voices and I was on, or rather the tape recorder was, my bit was all pre-recorded. This put me in the bizarre and unique position of being in the audience and 'on' stage at the same time. I'll never forget sitting in the front row and the surge of emotion when my voice came on. Tears trickled down my face as I witnessed myself performing live professionally for the first time.

Payment was two free tickets, but it was experience and that's what the budding actress and media person is always looking for. It also led to more work with that particular company and I felt it brought me closer to getting that elusive Equity card.

In the meantime, though, I was still in Bristol and trying to get a degree. The end of my final year was looming and I had exams to pass. I spent most of my third year working on my three special topics – slavery, satire and Virgil and, of course, the dreaded dissertation which contributed significantly enough to warrant thorough research. Any spare time was spent trying to make inroads into Radio Bristol. The day finally arrived when I had completed my Finals and I vowed that I would never take another exam, except possibly a Drama exam, and I have never broken my vow. After all that work and anxiety I came away with an honours degree in Classics, class 2.2. I was disappointed that it had not been a 2.1 but nobody in our year got a First. I cried about my grade, which in retrospect was quite absurd as it has not had one iota of relevance to any area of my life since, but at least it was over.

'Most of my time has been spent applying for jobs. Needless to say, I haven't got anything yet,' I wrote to Rosie in 1980. 'I registered at two agencies to increase my chances, but they go on about the recession, it's so depressing. I had an interview for the one job I really wanted, as a draughtswoman in the art department of a printing firm, and was very upset when I did not get it . . . so I rang the regional manager and asked why. He said there were other applicants with experience. Well he needn't have invited me for an interview in the first place and wasted my time.' I never was one to mince my words.

I had a few other interviews, including one more suited to my vocal talent, a part-time telephone canvassing job. 'I was keen to get it but had a letter turning me down . . . However, the interviewer sent me an unofficial letter along with the official one, saying he thought it important for me to know that the person who got the job had eight years' telesales experience and I was closer to getting it than I thought! As if that's any comfort!'

One evening I met an actor, Miles Anderson, at a first night party at the Bristol Old Vic. He said he would speak to someone in the B.B.C. who would arrange for me to read some stories. This led to the chance to talk to a Radio Bristol producer who said he was vastly impressed with my two demo cassettes (which I'd made with my drama teacher) and gave me an opportunity to watch his Sunday morning programme go out. 'I was very excited, despite the fact that I had to be there at 8.45 a.m., a time when I'm always fast asleep on a Sunday,' I wrote to Rosie. 'It was quite an experience being behind the scenes of a programme and the atmosphere was very casual, for instance the producer didn't turn up until 9.15 a.m., half an hour after I arrived. He kept on phoning with messages that he was stuck in bed!'

There were two studios separated by a glass panel, with the presenter on one side and the production team on the other. I enjoyed my time in the presenter's studio but I spent most of the programme in the control studio with the producer. It was pleasant but hardly anyone spoke to me. At the time I thought this was rather impolite but having since worked in broadcasting I realise that nobody has the time to talk! At the end of the programme the producer said he would speak to the person who was in charge of stories. He obviously kept his word, as I did get a chance to read some stories for Radio Bristol, which was very exciting. On the day, surprisingly, I wrote to Rosie: 'I didn't feel at all nervous, so the old adrenalin wasn't going!' I went on, 'Something rather good happened when I was at Radio Bristol. I had been told to ask if I could speak to the man who produces a programme for disabled people. By an incredible stroke of luck I met the bloke as I went into Radio Bristol and he asked me if I'd ever thought of being a presenter, and he wants me to present his programme!!' Strangely, though, I didn't hear from him until some time later when I was invited to give a speech at a wine reception for the launching of a fundraising campaign for a riding centre for the disabled.

'All these photographers were taking photos of me,' I wrote to Rosie, 'but I didn't appear in the *Evening Post*; David Broome did though. This bloke from Radio Bristol's disabled programme was there and he got me to do this pointless interview all about the new riding centre and whether I could manage everything myself. Well, the centre isn't even built yet, how am I supposed to know?! Half the time I just pretended to be really confident about things I couldn't possibly know. I did that because I've learnt that interviewers don't care *what* you say, all they want is an immediate, non-thought-out answer. He made me speak unnaturally fast and after the interview he went on about me arguing with him at Radio Bristol. I haven't a clue what he was on about. I kept saying to him, "What do you mean? What arguments?" but he would not explain himself . . . I had been really keen about presenting his programme, so I don't see where arguments come into it. Actually the whole evening was a bit of a farce as far as I was concerned, because all these horsey people are so involved and I'm not at all. I felt a bit of a fraud because in my speech I was going on about the importance of riding for disabled people and saying deep things about society and independence and stuff and I only went riding at university for a break from work.'

It was easy to feel at that time, despite the occasional function, that nothing was happening. I had hoped to be living away from home by then and I finally agreed to my parents buying me a duvet for Christmas in anticipation of such a move. I had received some very unpleasant hot water bottle burns and a duvet seemed the answer, as it was both warmer and easier for me to make my bed if I lived by myself. I was reading about a Christian quadriplegic, Joni Eareckson, at the time and I was so involved in her story that I had to ration myself to a chapter a day because I thought I would starve emotionally when it ended. I totally related to her and was going through the experiences I was reading. I was getting increasingly depressed and cried every day. Once again it was letters to Rosie that provided some release: 'I've been having a real helluva time. I've been going through emotional traumas and getting awfully depressed. My mother has been terribly nice to me, comforting me and trying to help. It's almost ironic really because I thought that after the end of my academic education nothing would be unbearable, whatever happened. But, in fact, with my future so uncertain and with so much time on my hands to think, I have been very unhappy. I've covered up to a considerable extent but when I've been by myself I've cried and cried.'

All the friends I had known at school or university had now left Bristol and, as I wrote to Rosie, I was feeling in limbo. However, I was not completely idle, and out of the doldrums of depression grew a totally unexpected bud that was to blossom and eventually bear fruit in a way surprising to many, not least myself. Like many people in similar circumstances I began to write, in my case poetry. At first I had no idea whether it was good enough for public consumption or whether it was worth carrying on with at all, but I confided in our lodger, Jim, who soon became my closest companion, and when I plucked up enough courage to show him a few poems he gave me that initial encouragement which is so vital to a budding writer. Without his assiduous watering of my seed I doubt very much if that first result would be publicly available today, and I don't underestimate the debt I owe to him for his part in a major turning point in my life. Around the same time, I gathered the nerve to write to the B.B.C. again, this time to Radio 1's *Studio B15* and I succeeded in getting another broadcast.

I had written to them to suggest I do a section in their programme on famous love poetry. They wrote back and said they thought it was a great idea and that I should prepare a structure for it. I was literally just finishing it off, having spent a lot of time on it, when the phone rang and *Studio B15* said, 'What we'd really like you to do is to interview Brian Patten, because he's a poet.' I was horrified. I had spent all this time preparing one thing and now they wanted me to do something else. I told them 'no'. The researcher attempted to persuade me but I was adamant, so she handed me over to her producer who used his charm on me. I succumbed, but for some inexplicable reason decided to take a poem or two of my own along – just in case.

The programme was chaired by Adrian Love who did the classic thing and said, 'The listeners won't know this, and I'm not saying this to embarrass you, but you are in fact in a wheelchair.' I don't usually mind that point being made so long as it is relevant to the discussion. In this case Adrian Love continued to mention his contacts with the Spastics Society and the fact that he kept going to weddings where one of the partners was in a wheelchair. He wondered whether this made any difference and I chipped in (desperate to get my voice on the radio), 'No, it makes no difference at all, um . . . What you said about it being surprising, that really shows or reflects society's attitude, or some people's attitudes, that if you're disabled then you're different inside. I'm no different inside from anyone else, so therefore my interest in love poetry isn't anything to do with my disability. The feelings are the same, after all.' Adrian Love asked me if I had one of my own poems with me. There followed a long pause while I scrabbled around looking for it and apologised for its quality. When I had read the poem Adrian was suitably complimentary and then Brian Patten was brought into the conversation to read some of his poetry. I hope I did not suffer too much in the comparison.

Drama lessons, lots of letter writing and occasional broadcasts had seemed like virtually no progress to me in those eighteen months in Bristol. But the theatre company for whom I had done those few brief voice-overs was forming a new cast so, early in 1981, I set off to London to start my acting career for real.

4

'The long and winding road . . .'
The Beatles

'I find it hard to believe I'm an actress. I feel a bit of a fraud sometimes, maybe because I've always wanted to be an actress and now that it's actually happened it's too amazing. I love the life and of course it's wonderful to be living away from home,' I wrote in April 1981 to Rosie. That year, 1981, was the International Year of Disabled People, or I.Y.D.P., and the company I had joined was 'The Theatre of the Disabled'. The name itself was a strange anachronism in a year dedicated to disabled people. It was 'the disabled' that was the problem. The disabled what? So I was slightly uncomfortable about working in a company with such a name. It sounded rather arrogant. Theatre of *the* disabled sounded a bit like theatre of *the* Black, implying that only black people or disabled people are worth watching perform. In fact the cast did try to get the name changed; we even bought T-shirts and had 'Raspberry Ripple' printed on them, but the founder of the company only replied that if we were having it changed to anything it would be 'The Theatre of Courage'. Talk about banging your head against a brick wall! That was even worse. We're not courageous, we're just getting on with being alive and, incidentally, disabled. The title 'Theatre of Courage' showed how little he really understood about living with a disability.

The company itself was set up by an able-bodied man

who wrote and produced his own plays as well as raising the money for them. In fact he wrote them under an assumed name so nobody realised that writer and producer were one and the same man. What we also did not realise was that he was obtaining funding for the company by writing begging, tear-jerking letters to Equity members asking them to put themselves in our place because we were disabled and so, he thought, unable to work. He used our disabilities rather than our talent to raise the money. At the time none of us knew about this and I was embarrassed when I found out about it from friends in Equity. I would like to think the producer's intentions for setting up the company were honourable but cynics would say that he used actors with disabilities to provide a platform for his own writing.

One of the most valuable aspects of my first professional engagement was the chance it gave me to learn my craft. I had wanted to go to the Bristol Old Vic Theatre School on their one-year post-graduate course but there were only three places – one female and two male – and I was virtually told not to bother to apply. If it had been me now I would have applied anyway, but I was more easily squashed in those days. Despite the fact that most actors say they learn the majority of skills after drama school, it is well nigh impossible to get a job without a recognised training. Thus the double disadvantage for disabled people wanting to join the acting profession, because we are generally not accepted into drama school in the first place.

Although, no doubt, I would have drawn the line somewhere, this was my first job and I was not about to miss the chance to leave home and enter the world of paid employment. Moreover, I thought it must be good because it was a professional engagement, but as time passed I more than once went through the 'I'm embarrassed to be in this show' phase and we all became bored with the script. Similarly, the novelty of touring wore off, but I had suspected that would happen. Still, on with the show!

When I left Bristol I asked one or two people to pray for me because I would now be working in a non-Christian environment. I thought it would be extra-tough in the world of theatre. As it happened, the other actresses on the tour turned out to be Christians themselves or verging that way. In fact Pete, the stage manager, remarked derogatively that we were the most religious crowd he had met, to which I replied, 'I'm not religious – at least, not in the way you mean.' In other words, I was unlikely to live up to his stereotype. On a more positive note, Pennie, the assistant stage manager (A.S.M.) expressed interest in religion and said that she envied those of us with faith. I remember one night on the road in our van when the conversation got deeply philosophical. At one a.m. I was about to go to sleep but felt I ought to contribute to the conversation. I don't make a concerted effort to Bible-bash people when I'm on tour, but when you are with the same people twenty-four hours a day I feel some sort of responsibility as a Christian. I wrote in my diary at the time that I did feel under pressure to show love at all times. It is easy to get impatient when you are living and working at such close quarters, and I felt I had to keep that under control because they knew I was a Christian, and should live up to certain standards.

When the company came across the more overt kind of witnessing, I felt my covert approach was justified. I remember once when we were in Scotland and staying at a Y.W.C.A. The place was full of 'No Smoking' signs and rules about not wearing see-through nighties. Going overboard on the Gospel tracts only added insult to injury. Pete said the place stank of Christianity and sexual repression which is an unfortunate connection, and he made bitter insinuating remarks about 'religion' again. Even Pennie said, 'It puts me off Christianity.' I felt angry. The Y.W.C.A. provided supper magnanimously, then charged an extra 50p each for it; when we did a bit of ironing, that was an extra 5p. It upset me to see the negative side of Christianity, which was so alien to my view.

Touring is a very up and down experience. I had been home for a few days' off and it was obvious to everyone I met how happy I was in my job; they said I had changed, was more positive. I looked very well and was radiant. One friend even said I had actress eyes. Yet the very next day after the show I wrote in my diary that it was the first time I was miserable since leaving home. There had been no response from the audience of seventeen in Surbiton and for the first time I wanted to finish the tour. Such is the life of an actor. We are often at the mercy of an audience so we can feel either deflated or elated after a night's work. During this tour I wrote a song about the more difficult aspects of touring which I sang three years later at the Edinburgh Festival.

Actress Eyes

actress eyes, actress eyes
she says I've got actress eyes
she says my eyes sparkle
she says my eyes shine
how do you do it she says
how do you do it?
I can't do that with mine

she doesn't know the price
she doesn't know the cost
what I've gained is less than I have lost
the friends I love I never see
desolation is part of me
what I contain is less than I've given
you know you lose your spark
you know you lose your style
when every hotel takes you further by the mile.
But you live for their praise
yes you live for their laughter and smiles
that makes your life worthwhile

actress cheek bones, actress cheek bones
she says I've got actress cheek bones
they highlight my face she says
they give me some style
well she can have them, my eyes my cheek bones
    my face
let's swap places for a while

Being flung together with people on the tour, and unable to escape, brought me to the rapid realisation that I needed time to myself because I was used to it. I had always had a good crowd of friends; in fact so many of them came to the shows that there was a standing joke in the company: 'Elly's been contacting "Rent a Friend" again.' But at the same time my disability had detracted from group activity; I had learned to love and need my own company at an early age. Once on tour, when Pennie commented she felt bad vibes coming from me, I was merely in a quiet state because the company was getting on top of me. Later, with another company, I revealed my rebellion in a letter home to Jim: 'I've already experienced, but resisted, the pressures of being greg-arious and falling in with the crowd, i.e. sitting up drinking all night. I made a point of immediately starting to write letters when we arrived and turning down demands of, "We'll see you in the bar, later" with replies like, "It depends whether I've finished my letter." That's produced comments like, "You must be the world's busiest correspondent." I think having flu has helped because I've had an excuse to rest which has been accepted by the crowd, especially with my voice being so vital to my work. I mean that's far less unreasonable than writing letters to people isn't it?'

I wrote in my diary, 'Touring puts you off chippies and Chinese take-aways for life.' Later, I wrote to Jim, 'I'll probably come back all spotty and grotty, or spottier and grottier than usual. I ate the most vile chicken pie and chips. The substance that posed as chicken probably never set foot in a farmyard. The next night I had coq au vin. The "coq" was an infinite improvement on the night before, though I couldn't detect the "vin" anywhere. My lunch feels like lead in my stomach. It was beefburgers from the bar.'

Acting with a wheelchair is a bit like acting with animals and children – it can be unpredictable. 'At Newcastle,' I wrote to Rosie, 'my chair started freaking out just before the curtain was going up. It started moving of its own accord. I collapsed in hysterics and Pennie, the A.S.M., phoned through to Pete in the lighting box and said, "Come quickly, Ellen's chair's gone wrong." He came and gave it some hard thumps to calm it down but I was terrified it might happen on stage and I would go flying over the edge!' Typically, the worst time when something went wrong for me with my wheelchair was when that actor's dream came true and a director was there in the audience to see my performance.

Some months before, I had been on a Graeae Theatre Company weekend workshop. Graeae Theatre Company is a company of professional actors with disabilities and it has established a very good reputation. It was on that weekend I met the company's co-founders, and its future director, Nic Fine. They kept in touch with me and asked me whether I would like to audition for their first professional show. By this time I was already committed to The Theatre of the Disabled so I had to say no. Well, if Mohammed cannot come to the mountain, the mountain must come to Mohammed and I had an audition *in situ* at one of my performances. As it happened, that was the night our own director came to the show and walked out on us halfway through, taking a whole group of friends with her, all because we had made a few changes in the show. That completely threw us. I had already burst into tears for making a fool of myself on stage by getting my skirt caught in the wheel of my chair. I wrote to Jim, 'It was, typically, the one night when it was vital for me to do everything right because my friend Nic, the director of Graeae, was there and talked to me about a job with them. I didn't know he was there until the interval when a man grabbed my hand and held it tight. It was Nic and I was embarrassed at not recognising him, because he had his beard and moustache shaved off. Of course that night there was a turmoil in my mind, not knowing what to do – whether Graeae actually wanted me to work for them. At the moment I feel I just can't look ahead and it doesn't help not knowing when this tour is going to end. I keep telling myself God will deal with it so there is no need to worry.' I also wrote at the end of that letter, 'The tour is changing me . . . it's for the better not for the worse and in a way that's imperceptible.' The entry in my diary for the same day explained: 'I've had all I want and now I want what God wants because He knows best. Before I kept back a bit.'

That is all very well when the going is good, as it was at the time. The *Leicester Mercury* said of us: 'I doubt a more moving production will grace Leicester's stage this year.' The Phoenix Theatre, where we had performed, said they had never seen such a good write-up. Even the review in *The Stage* was not bad despite my conviction that it would be. The reviewer had been combing his hair all through the performance. When he asked for a programme, our company manager said, 'Sure, 10p please' to which he replied, 'Oh, for goodness' sake, I am from *The Stage*, you know!'

Most of the time we got on very well on tour, had a lot of good laughs together and built up strong bonds. Yet touring is a tough and draining experience even for the most resilient like myself. The times when I was ill with flu, laryngitis or worse took the edge off my excitement and detracted from my enjoyment of a generally very happy experience. I had to do one performance mouthing the words while the rest of the company sang my song. After a night in a depressing venue I described it to Jim as: 'dirty and miserable enough to put the most dedicated actor off acting for life. I've got every reason to be happy, so what's wrong with me? I put it down to being physically low. It's a vicious circle. The less sleep I get the worse I feel physically, then the worse I feel mentally and I begin to lose more sleep thinking of all the things on my mind at night.'

The problem with touring in fringe theatre is the impossibility of taking time off to recuperate and thus any illness is exacerbated, as I pointed out to Jim: 'I went to the doctor the day before yesterday because everyone said I looked tired, and the company manager was concerned and said I ought to see a doctor. It was the most hilarious visit. We all went in together and we kept on laughing and joking. He got the wrong end of the stick and wrote on my card that I'd had diarrhoea on and off for a year since a trip to France. That's because I told him, in answer to various questions, that I'd been in St Lucia a year ago, bought some medicine in France last summer and had had diarrhoea on and off for three weeks. I tried to point out to him that I'd only been ill for three weeks but he just looked at me, smiled and carried on writing to my doctor. I may have a tropical disease called "giardia". On the other hand, the problem may be caused by stress – what did I tell you? I'm taking more care of myself now, though not as much as the doctor would like. You know, just miss a few performances and, if it carries on, miss a few months of the tour!'

I believe that many bookings arose as a result of the International Year of Disabled People. Disability was flavour of the year and some venues booked us who otherwise would have passed us by. We played at Islington Town Hall once, which had slipped my memory until I lived in London and then I remembered the Mayoress wanting to stop the performance halfway through and run a raffle. We had a wide range of audiences and some hilarious occasions such as old dears knitting and singing in the front row. We even did one open air performance in Warrington Park, or at least half a performance. We cancelled the second half due to the rain. It was a farce anyway, with young lads talking all the way through.

The major venue of the tour had to be the Dominion

Theatre for The Royal Command Performance before Prince and Princess Michael of Kent. Other performers included Elaine Paige, Dickie Henderson, Iris Williams and Harry Secombe. One of our cast got terribly worried about being presented to the royals with one spot on her face so we teased her, saying that they would not notice her because of it.

The party after the performance showed up the pretentious side of the theatre world which I found very difficult to handle. On more than one occasion this made me want to leave the profession. My mother once said about herself, 'I am no good at superficial conversation,' and, taking after my mother in this respect, I once told a friend in a conversation how meaningless clichés were. He said it was nice if a friend used a cliché which captured how he felt. I told him, 'I never feel like a cliché. I would rather a friend was honest with me than used a cliché that might be inaccurate, supposedly to comfort me. I can't believe they are genuine if they use a cliché.' Similarly, theatre people could leave me cold, but even this party had a highlight. Harry Secombe came over and gallantly got down on his knees to kiss me goodbye, and in the process spilt my gin and tonic over me. Ever the gentleman, he pulled out his neatly folded white handkerchief from his breast pocket and, amidst profuse apologies, dried the damage and gave me the hanky to keep (unused of course). He signed it, 'To Ellie, love Harry Secombe'. I told him it was worth getting my drink spilt for that. I was nicknamed Ellie in the theatre and stuck to it for my Equity performing name. It does cause confusion because I stick to Ellen for writing, singing and poetry performances.

Really the most memorable performance, and one of the most incredible experiences of my life, was in Edinburgh prison. We were given Jimmy Boyle's cell to use as our backstage area. There were so many innocent faces, I couldn't believe that they were criminals. We were shown round the prison and lots of the men talked to me. One said how he wished more females would come to the prison because they never get a female point of view. He went on to tell me how hard it would be to build up a relationship again after he got out. The relaxed atmosphere, with so many of them willing to talk, was not what I had expected.

The prisoners were a receptive audience as well as being a 'captive' audience. We were not the only performers that day. The prison band, aptly named 'The Forgotten Few', played for us in return and I cried inside when one sang, 'Hallelujah freedom, freedom day, Hallelujah freedom, freedom way'. The words were obviously heartfelt. To my great surprise and disbelief, one prisoner gave me a painting he had done. It was this experience and this man, John, that were to lead me to take a more active interest in prisons and prisoners. No wonder one of our company said she had never seen me so animated as in the prison.

In the meantime I had a decision to make about Graeae. I was by now tired out by months of touring and needed a holiday on a sunny island somewhere. Were I to join Graeae, I would have to go straight into another tour. But before I knew for sure that there was a job waiting for me with Graeae, there was talk of another tour for the Theatre of the Disabled. The producer wanted a commitment and I was forced to say 'I am with you a hundred per cent'. The next day, when I rang Nabil in Graeae to get Nic's address and write to him, he told me the good news that Nic had been very impressed with my acting and wanted me to be the sixth member of the company for the Edinburgh Festival. Then I had the dilemma of what to tell my present producer, but I left that to God and didn't worry at that stage. I was in fact under no legal obligation to him.

Although the job with Graeae was a marvellous opportunity, I was not at peace about accepting it. I had actually prayed not to get the job because I would have no holiday. Then, confused, I felt it must be right to go to Graeae, otherwise God would not have let me get the job. It seemed miraculous that Graeae wanted me at all. I spent two hours trying to pluck up the courage to write a letter informing my present producer of my new job, but I sat there with pen and paper unable to write more than a paragraph and I never finished it. It was like one of those dreams where you are being chased and your legs are paralysed. I simply did not feel happy about going for the Graeae job at this stage. I cried on the telephone to my mother for an hour because I felt awful at having to back out of a job I had accepted, but without a break I would not be fit enough to give my best and if I was going to do it at all I wanted to do it well. In the end, I rang Nic and told him so. I expected him to be annoyed but on the contrary he quite understood, much to my relief. Mind you, I knew there was no guarantee that I would ever get another offer.

Near the end of the tour I was amazed when Chris Harris, an actor with the Old Vic, came backstage. I was just about to say 'I know you' when he said, 'I know you'. I was very taken aback because I had never spoken to him and wondered how he could distinguish me from Eve. I obviously knew him from Adam because he was an established actor whom I had seen perform. It was a magic moment for me due to the association with my 'home' theatre.

On the last night we somehow got talking about religion again. Pete said, 'If you could get rid of religion, people would be much nicer.' I said, 'Thanks,' and told him he was making sweeping statements and pointed out the basis of Christianity was love and peace. I tried to make the point that he should not look at the Church but at Christ in people, but I'm not sure my point was clear because – well – it was the last night and I'd had a lot to drink!

I possibly suffered tour withdrawal symptoms in the summer because I wrote to Jim saying I had 'nothing else to do' but assist a theatre company called Breadrock by talking to their audiences. Well, I went to the venue, hung around for an hour, bought a grotty hot dog and then came home as I couldn't find anyone. I told Jim in disgust, 'Talk about Breadrock, there was not a crumb or pebble in sight.'

I went on holiday to Holland with my friend, Helena, and had a great time youth hostelling and eating Dutch pastries. That holiday vastly improved my frame of mind. 'I'm having just about the best holiday ever, Holland is better than all my holidays in France put together. I prefer the Van Gogh museum to the Rijksmuseum where lots of famous Rembrandts are, and to the Stedelijk Museum where lots of rubbishy modern artists are. There was one room where each exhibit moved (except the one that was *defunkt* when you pressed a button on the floor, e.g. a pile of old rusty metal on a dustbin went up and down. It was quite disturbing to see things like bundles of rags stuck on walls in a modern art museum, I could have done it myself and people wouldn't pay to see it. Holland is a juicy country, lush and green with canals and windmills, I am in love with Amstersdam.

I returned home with the hope of the planned second tour with The Theatre of the Disabled but it fell through, and I was back to square one – or so I thought.

5

*'I've been on the road so long my friend, and if you
came along I know you wouldn't disagree'*
Simon and Garfunkel

'When my contract ended I got a job,' I wrote to Rosie in
October 1981. 'It happened all of a sudden, but it's
worked out very well and I'm happy again. To start from
the beginning . . . I got back from Holland and felt
terribly miserable when I found my last friend had left
Bristol and of course I had no job to look forward to,
either. Then a friend invited me to Harrogate for a
weekend and I only just arrived back when my friend
Nic, director of Graeae, rang me to say they were looking
for a replacement for one of their actors, but he didn't
think I was right for the part and in any case they hadn't
got time to look for accommodation or transport for me
because they needed their replacement to start the
following week.'

There were difficulties with following up this new
glimmer of hope from Graeae, but I had had my holiday
now and was really determined not to let another opportunity pass me by. In the end I managed to persuade Nic
to consider me for the job if I could overcome all the
practical difficulties. Then I had the problem of finding
somewhere to live and someone to drive me in a strange
town. It was not easy. I really thought I had no chance of
getting the job, but in my excited letter to Rosie I went on,
'Then a miracle happened. I went to tea with friends of

the family and there met a guy whose parents live in Farnborough, right next door to Aldershot (where Graeae is based). Well, to cut a long story short, he got on the phone to his mother and she very kindly offered me a room in her house and said she would find me transport. She wouldn't let me pay for the first week I was there. They're a Christian family so I guess they do it out of love.' Anyway, after finding accommodation, I phoned Nic who said that Graeae would now consider me for the job. To my amazement I got it but I only had one day to pack and get everything ready. I had arranged to go out all that day so had a massive panic, literally throwing things in a bag. My Dad got quite annoyed and said, 'I'm taking this bag, ready or not,' and then muttered something about me getting a taxi. So a day later, after all the agonising and refusal of a few months before, I was finally working for Graeae.

The name 'Graeae' refers to three sisters in Greek mythology who shared one eye and a tooth between them and so were forced to work as a team. Their disabilities were also exploited by Perseus. The only problem with such an esoteric name was that no one could pronounce it if they saw it, or spell it if they heard it, so we were called all sorts of wild and wonderful things like 'Green Eye' and 'Grey Owl'.

I loved my work, even though it was hyper-hectic at first and I only had four days of rehearsals before my first performance due to taking over the part while the company were in mid-tour. After the first day at work I wrote in my journal: 'Supposed to work 10 a.m. to 5 p.m. Still there after 6.30. Absolutely exhausted. A hundred and one things to do. I should have learned pages of lines I've not started! I love it though. The atmosphere and people are lovely. This company's going to be a real laugh. Nic calls me "darling" like a true theatrical.'

We were touring two shows, *Sideshow* and *3D*, both on the theme of disability. *3D* was a biographical dramatisation of the cast members' life stories, so it was some time before I performed in this play because a new tailor-made

71

part was required. This involved sessions of spouting about my life and contributing to the script. I received a back-handed compliment from the writer of the play and co-founder of the company, Richard Tomlinson: he said I was, 'difficult to write with because I was too educated and logical and wrote too well myself'.

My predecessor in the company had been Nabil Shaban, also a co-founder of Graeae and an actor who was establishing a good reputation for himself. I was more than a little apprehensive about following in his footsteps, but I was cheered up after my debut performance when a man said he would never have known it was my first night. I was ill with gastric flu at the time, as well. At some venues I disappointed people who were expecting Nabil, but I had my compensatory compliments such as, 'Your face is so expressive. You made me cry and I never cry!'

Graeae was far more than a good chance to improve my acting skill. All sorts of issues would come up in the pub, including the old taboos of religion, death and sex. I found it hard the way sex was debased by referring to intercourse with very crude terminology. I was never prim and proper but I had a more holistic approach to sex which affected my use of language.

I also worked through a number of things that bothered me. One day, in the pub after lunch, Nic and I had a long and intense talk about relationships because I said I felt I was a burden to people and I was very aware of it and hated people having to do things for me. Nic pointed out the necessity to be assertive in certain situations. I replied, 'I can't, because firstly I feel so bad, and secondly I think it will make things worse. Thirdly I feel I should accept people as they are.'

Graeae was tougher than the previous theatre company in some ways. When I said I was apolitical they told me I was wet. It was certainly through Graeae that I became politicised, and I am referring to disability politics not party politics. Because my upbringing and education had been totally integrated for twenty-one years, I had never mixed with disabled people. A political movement was irrelevant to my lifestyle at this stage. It was only when I started working with other disabled people, and fighting my own battles outside the comfort of home, that I could feel solidarity with them.

It would be wrong of me to pretend I didn't have a privileged upbringing, but that by no means prevents me from genuinely supporting and identifying with the disability movement now. I recognise that my childhood didn't give me a burning need to channel anger in a positive political way. I did not experience the oppression of grim institutions, nor was I dished up a diluted education. Interestingly, I was once accused of not being very involved in the disability movement, which is an unfair attack; the politics of disability are important to my life, as it is to those deeply involved with the movement itself, but I choose to work in my own quiet way. There is a danger with any political movement of leaders becoming dictators and imposing the terms of involvement. Individuals may have their own political reasons for their actions and, if it happens not to be in line with the current trend, are they less involved members?

When I was not working I was really living it up. One night I was so tired I fell asleep before I lay down properly and I woke up in the middle of the night with a tube of cream in one hand and the top of the tube in the other. Among other things, working with Graeae gave me a chance to sing quite a bit and I was informed that my 'Cripple Through the Door' song in the show was excellent. That sort of remark makes an actor feel like a million dollars but I wasn't going to let it go to my head. However, given the path my performing career was later to go along, compliments like that are quite significant. At a London girls' school they gave us a standing ovation as if we were royalty. I had never heard such applause, it gave me a lump in my throat. We were told at lunch time that the girls never stood up for anyone.

Touring with Graeae was always eventful. One night we ended up stranded in a snow storm on our way to

Norwich. We got as far as Cambridge and that was only in the nick of time before the town was cut off by snow. We were put up for the night by the Social Services in a new home for mentally disabled people that had not yet opened so the wing was brand new. I felt like a refugee because the floor was covered with people, and more and more kept pouring in.

Looking at my diary now I notice that I did things like go to bed at two in the morning and get up five hours later at seven. No wonder I was tired. I couldn't do that now. As with all tours, there were fantastic highs and real lows. We did a show before an audience of eight hundred in Aberdeen's Beach Ballroom but in Leicester we finished up in a dingy hotel. It had six-inch mushrooms and pink mould growing up the lavatory wall, and a sulky chambermaid who brought breakfast with the greeting, 'You might move your bag so people can get in'. Mind you, there were some people I definitely wanted to keep out. I wrote in my diary, 'There's a drunk Scotsman outside my room using the phone. He just peed outside the door, I thought it was raining. "I'm sober noo," he says. He's talking about his sexual conquests. Help! He's trying to get into my room.' I switched off the light and did not move.

One of the most nerve-racking venues for me was the performance on home ground in Bristol, because I knew my parents, friends and ex-drama teacher were all there. I made quite a few mistakes and nearly burst into tears when I got caught up in the fairy crown, but still managed to impress people and my dad threw me a bouquet of flowers at the curtain call. It was something I had always yearned for in my 'actress dream', but once it happened in reality I was so overwhelmed I didn't know which way to turn. What a berk!

One of the major highlights was a week in France for a festival of theatre by actors with disabilities. It had its frustrations but was a fantastic experience.

'To France, October 27th 1981 – arrived Calais. They won't let us through Customs because English Customs have not stamped our form. Sue (the stage manager) went straight back to England on the next boat just to get the form stamped. Meanwhile Jean Marc talked to the Customs and tried to get us through. In the end, instead of Jean Marc taking us to Lille, we paid to spend the night in a hotel in Calais, called the Hotel Bristol (ironic). Customs allowed us through with the van so long as we came back by 7.45 a.m. the next day with the signed form . . . Crazy. They let us through only to come back. It's illogical. In the night Sue came back to get the van because the English Customs would not sign the form without the van! Sue arrived in Calais unable to find the van, which she thought was not allowed through Customs. In the end the French Customs allowed us through without the form signed. It was a total farce. Our hotel rooms were all on the top floor and an angry Frenchman came and shouted at us as a fellow actress was carried upstairs in her wheelchair!'

That week continued in much the same vein. It was all very disorganised. We never received the schedule which they insisted they sent, but nobody knew what was happening or when, anyway. On the first day we went to the theatre to rehearse with the French director, Luc, but he wasn't there and when someone fetched him, he appeared for literally ten seconds then dashed off, never to return that day. I wrote in my journal for October 29th, 'Rehearsal with elusive French director. Spent the day waiting for French T.V. crew, which never arrived. Farce again. At the end of the afternoon we were told to go to the director's office for T.V. We had just got there, got our wheelchairs up a flight of stairs, which was a big hassle, and then Luc turned round and said, ''T.V. aren't coming. Be here 9.30 a.m. tomorrow.'' We felt very cheesed off. It was beyond a joke by then.'

However, after all that, our performance at L'Opéra Lille, where Edith Piaf did her last performance, went down very well. It was special for me to perform there as I am an admirer of Piaf and happened to be reading her biography at the time.

Soon after our return from France a shock was in store for me. I was told I had to move out of my accommodation as my landlady was going to hospital. I found somewhere temporarily, but it was not ideal as I had to share a room and had no privacy, which is important to me. So I still had to spend time looking for an alternative and the only option that materialised was a room in a convent. The trouble was that the nuns wanted someone to be there with me. By this time, being unhappy where I was living had taken its toll and I was on edge so I asked Nic to bear with me at work. He was kind enough to tell me I was the least irritable of the company, which eased my mind.

I went home to Bristol for Christmas and New Year with no definite accommodation arranged. I rang the convent to see about my room but the nuns said I could not have it as my own permanent room. Each time I went on tour I would have to pack all my things away as if the room belonged to no one. I was shattered. I desperately wanted a place of my own more than anyone could know. I wrote in my diary for the 11th of January, 'So depressed re. accommodation and volunteers. Everywhere I go a dead end. No replies to the advert, no luck with a volunteer from the Rushmore Centre. Phoned the Social Services and asked them for a home help. "No!" Asked them to find accommodation – "NO". GIVE UP!'

However, a week later the convent had changed their mind again and I was very happy in my own place. I wrote in my diary, 'For the first time in my life I prepared, ate and washed up and dried my own meal. Found independence at last.' Living there produced some amusing reactions; some local children were surprised I went to a disco because they thought I lived in a church and was a nun.

The convent was not to be a permanent arrangement, since I had their only spare room. I certainly learned the skill of flat-hunting which is not something I expected to learn from the acting profession. This time I approached the Shaftesbury Society who had some sheltered accommodation in Aldershot. I went to see one of their empty flats to assess its suitability. I became angry and upset at the number of objections people kept raising. I was a young woman by now and people were still telling me I wasn't physically capable of things I knew I could do. They might just as well have stood there and told me I didn't know my own body. I was very determined.

The following day one of the nuns came and told me that the Shaftesbury Society man had been very impressed with my determination and if anything was going to get me the flat, that would. The flat had to be adapted for my special needs (this mainly means lower everything – door handles, taps, etc – so that it all comes within my reach). The Shaftesbury Society wanted me to promise them that I would live in it for two years, in order to justify the expense of adapting the flat. Anyone who knows anything about acting will know what an unrealistic requirement this was. I could have been anywhere in the next two years, as indeed I was. Graeae assured me, as far as they could, that all things being equal I would be on the team for a while yet. My father acted as guarantor, should I have to renege on the agreement. In the end I did have to leave before the statutory two years were up but one of the new Graeae actors desperately needed accommodation so the Society did not spend extra money making the alterations. Thus my father did not have to honour the guarantee either, thankfully.

Apart from putting in a phone, which is as vital to me as water is to flowers, the first thing I did when I got into the flat was have a flat warming party – not essential but very desirable. However, the experience of post-party-clear-up is not so pleasant, so I was grateful that my brother Alcuin and two friends had stayed overnight because the next day we eliminated the wine stains and cigarette ash and disposed of two boxes of rubbish. Unfortunately, the party had not gone unnoticed by my neighbours, who were mainly elderly. The next day the warden scolded me like a naughty schoolgirl: 'Miss Wilkie, have you read the rulebook?'

'Yes'

'Well, did you notice it said no noise after 11 p.m.?'

'Oh no, I didn't read that one.' (Neither did I find it in the rule book when I read it later.) The warden said he had heard people leaving at 4.15 a.m. and that the alarm cord in the loo had been pulled twice at 1.30 a.m. I had warned people about that but the panic cord was right next to the loo and people obviously mistook it for the flush. It was all very embarrassing. It may be convenient to house old people and young disabled people together, but there is still a generation gap to be crossed.

The round of acting, socialising and hassles continued. I had a night of hilarity in Dundee. To start with, we were expecting five bedrooms between our company of eight and we were only allocated two. I slept on the floor in a living-room and managed to get locked in. Luckily there was an internal phone in the room which I could reach from the floor, so I picked up the receiver and told the voice on the other end I was locked in and I couldn't reach the latch and didn't know where I was! I didn't even know the street name because that sort of thing is not important on tour. It's just a room for the night. I got handed over to a Scotsman and couldn't understand what he was saying. By this time I couldn't stop laughing and was worried they would think I was only messing around. I don't recollect telling them some things like why I was there or that I was disabled. But a porter finally arrived to set me free.

On our opening night at the Riverside Studios in Hammersmith I was so nervous I spent an hour and a half on the loo, but the performance went well in the theatre and we had rave reviews in *The Times*, the *Financial Times*, the *Guardian* and the *Daily Telegraph* whose critic Eric Shorter said, 'There isn't a moment's monotony or sentimentality. There is instead much humour, some wit and a most persuasive sincerity in these reported experiences of what it is like to have cerebral palsy or muscular dystrophy or to have arms which won't reach across your chest or to dread the loss of your sight.'

On the third night a fellow graduate from the Classics Department at Bristol was in the audience and came backstage afterwards. I had never socialised or even chatted with him and he had always appeared a buttoned up, unemotional type, but with tears in his eyes he thanked me for the show and said it had opened his eyes and was wonderful.

The end of the tour was in sight and, like all actors, I would soon be 'resting'. On the last night it was terrible saying goodbye to everyone. My sadness brought me to the verge of tears. When Nic said, 'It's not the end of an old life, but the beginning of a new life,' I replied, 'But I don't like the new life.'

My paid work being at an end for the moment, I had to sign on. Due to my disability I was not expected to wheel myself down to the dole office, partly because many of these offices are inaccessible to wheelchairs, so the D.H.S.S. (as it was called then) fixed an appointment to come and assess me at home – or least that was what was supposed to happen.

'Friday June 25th. Back to Aldershot. Flipping Social Security didn't turn up. Felt cheesed off and miserable, but too cold and tired to do anything. That was the only reason I'd gone back. I could have stayed longer with Deniz in London if it wasn't for the Social Security.'

Deniz was a fellow-actor in Graeae and we spent quite a bit of time together. Once when we went out for an Italian meal I got my ring stuck in the fishnet draping on the wall. Deniz was tugging and left a great gaping hole in the fishnet and I nearly fell off the chair laughing. Deniz came back that night and slept on the floor and we further disgraced ourselves by spilling cider on the carpet. It was my convent period and I was terrified the nuns would find out.

My financial situation was not eased by the D.H.S.S. forgetting their appointment. Red bills and threats to cut me off were now flowing in along with a letter from the D.H.S.S. informing me of my next appointment (Monday, June 28th), but of course I wasn't going to be there. I had already arranged to be in Bristol by Sunday, June 27th, when I went to church and heard a sermon on 'Hope amidst Despair' but it did not give me much hope. The final blow was in store: 'Friday 13th (August). Unluckiest day of my life. No job with Graeae.'

6

'History repeats itself
Has to
No one listens'
Steve Turner

'I have just come back from the most incredible holiday ever!' or so I wrote in the summer 1980 edition of the *Muscular Dystrophy Journal* where my journalism career began. I had gone to visit my brother and sister-in-law in St Lucia, on my first major trip beyond Europe by myself. It was a big event and I wrote on a postcard to Rosie: 'I was so excited and emotional before getting on the plane that I had a lump in my throat. Paul McCartney travelled on the same flight and I just missed him going on.'

What struck me immediately was how friendly everybody was. When we drove from the airport I was amazed at how many people shouted 'Hello' or waved at us as we went past (I thought my brother had a lot of friends) and they continued to be that friendly throughout the holiday. They acted as people in England would act only if they knew you well. They were not only friendly however, they were also curious. At first I thought they were insensitive as many of them asked my brother if I was sick or how long I had been like it. Could I talk, feed myself and so on? The questions were endless. Each time we went out we were bombarded by the curious. I wouldn't have minded so much if they had asked me the questions and not acted as if I were a nincompoop who could not hear or understand what they were saying. After a while, though, I relaxed. I began to realise they were just uninhibited and interested. They simply wanted to know, and perhaps by giving voice to their curiosity they became better informed than most people are over here. Some of the conversations were quite funny: on one occasion, in the same minute, I was mistaken first for my brother's daughter and then for his grandmother.

It was my first experience of a really different culture. Never had I imagined being able to see so many palm trees together in one place. I loved to watch the old men sitting outside their houses by a wood fire, or in groups by the roadside with mysterious looks on their faces and playing dominoes, or just talking. When I went to the beach for the first time I just sat there for half an hour taking in my surroundings: the white sand, the calm blue sea and more palm trees. Every now and then I would exclaim, 'Wow, this is amazing, I can't believe I'm really here.' I must admit, however, that if my sister-in-law had bought her meat from the market I would have turned vegetarian. In among the tables piled high with baskets, brooms and mats there were stalls serving food and drink, and dirty cubicles where men were hacking away at unpromising pieces of meat with what looked like old axes. These were probably the cutlasses which were used by everyone for everything from cutting toenails to cutting the grass.

The end of that holiday came all too soon but not my taste for travel. I had broken the border barrier and flown solo, so now the world was my oyster. However, as with all feelings of triumph, sometimes the reality proves much more difficult to achieve.

My next major trip was to the U.S.A. in 1983. An organisation called Mobility International, based in America, was running its first combined work camps for able-bodied and disabled people. It was the first camp of its kind and since I am ever the pioneer I applied to go. I was the only applicant from the U.K. so they were very pleased to have me and all I had to do was book the flight.

Easy enough, you may think, considering I had flown before, but here began a controversy on a par with that which I had experienced when I tried to return to the Sixth Form at school.

Whenever I book a flight I always tell the travel agent or the airline what my requirements are. They are in fact, very simple; for instance, I need help to get to the loo, so it's usually best to park me near to it so that the stewards and stewardesses have minimum work to do on my behalf. However, despite the fact that I always do inform the airline of my needs, and despite these days of computer information, I invariably get to the airport to discover that no one is expecting a passenger in a wheelchair. This happened when my friend, Helen, and I were returning from a holiday in Greece. The seating plans had been muddled, and we found a middle-aged couple in our seats. We were informed that we should wait until everyone had sat down and then fill the spare seats, but these turned out to be in the front row where disabled people are not allowed to sit because they are next to emergency exits. If the theory behind this rule is that we don't block the exits, it is laughable – what better place for us to sit should we need to get out in a hurry? Somehow I don't see people struggling to carry me down several crowded and panic-stricken aisles to get me to the exit, obstructing others as we go. It would be far more effective to put the disabled nearest the exit so that the least effort could be expended in getting us out. The ruling basically assumes that no help would be offered to disabled people and therefore they should be placed where it would be easy to leave them behind.

In any case, waiting for spare seats is not that simple for me. When I sit in a plane seat, because I don't have much strength in my back and because there is often no support for my feet to compensate for that, I am sort of pitched forward and I often go to sleep with my head resting against the seat in front. This is not comfortable – but then who is on a plane? Neither is it painful so it does until the time comes to eat. Then I do need some help. I can't have my tray placed in front of me so I usually share the person's next to me and we eat in turns. This is why I needed to sit next to Helen.

While we waited for everyone to settle down, I sat in the remaining seat next to the couple. Apart from other single seats, there was finally only space at the back of the plane, and I decided to stick to the principle of the thing. It was the airline's mistake, why should I move? Especially since moving further back down the plane would entail Helen lifting me up above the heads of all the passengers and carrying me down the aisle in a conspicuous and ungraceful manner, knickers flashing. However, the wife of the couple refused to move, neither did she want to be separated from her husband because she was afraid of flying. I realise that integration means mucking in with everyone else but a little consideration is not a high price to pay and for people who can walk, swapping seats is not a major physical hassle. The airline staff could have solved the problem by finding other seats for them and politely asking them to move down the plane.

In the end, I sat next to the couple and Helen found a seat elsewhere until lunchtime when she and the husband swapped seats. At some point during these musical chairs, the woman needed to go to the loo. As she clambered over me she slightly twisted her leg and there was a great to-do about that. In the event she did not come back to her seat but found somewhere else to sit with her husband, which had been the obvious thing to do in the first place.

It wasn't the most pleasant flight back, but I comfort myself with the thought that it reflected more detrimentally on the airline and the couple than it did on me. It turned out that the woman had been nicknamed Mrs Moaner (M.M. for short) by her fellow travellers on her package.

However that little incident was not a patch on what I had to deal with in my battle with the Northwest Orient Airline to fly to America in 1983.

Like most people going on holiday, especially to some-where expensive like the States, I wanted the cheapest flight I could find. I looked in the cheap flights section of the *Evening Standard* in London and rang a travel agency that was advertising attractive prices. I told the agent about my disability and when I was asked whether I had any special needs I asked to be seated in an aisle seat and said I needed a little help in getting to the loo. I was told this would be no problem, and that they had already organised help for the stopover and for going through Customs and Immigration.

I was booked on the flight on the 2nd of June with Northwest Orient Airlines. Two days later I was asked to provide a medical certificate which stated that I was fit to travel. I was not asked for anything else. My doctor wrote: 'Miss Ellen Wilkie is perfectly fit to travel and fly abroad and has done so many times before.' My doctor, in fact, thought it was all an excellent idea.

Then suddenly I was informed that I was not to absorb any food or liquid for twelve hours before departure, that I would not be allowed to swallow anything during the flight and that I should either have a catheter or wear a nappy. Northwest Orient also told me that they would not take responsibility for me during a twelve-hour wait for a connecting flight, neither would they wheel me through Customs or Immigration.

I rang Northwest Orient and I spoke to someone called Cathy who told me that their staff union rules were that they could not lift any passenger during the flight. What if someone dropped dead or was taken ill? I wondered. I was advised to ring the station manager at Gatwick Airport, from where the flight would start. It took me a long time to get through, partly because the actual station manager was absent. The man I spoke to was the acting station manager. By this time I had been on the phone for several days trying to persuade Northwest Orient that I would be no trouble and needed minimum care. I had also had to inform Mobility International, who told me that this situation could not arise in America as the company would be obliged to take me. The whole thing was costing me a fortune in phone bills. I asked the station manager at Gatwick on what grounds Northwest Orient made their ruling about not lifting passengers. He could only reply that that was their union rule.

'But why?' I asked.

'I don't know. Maybe because of the liability of dropping or rupturing.' I offered to provide a written disclaimer not charging them with any fault if they dropped me.

'But what if the crew member ruptures his or her back lifting you? He or she could sue you,' said Mr Drury.

'But I only weigh four stone.'

'Ah, that's fifty-six pounds, Miss Wilkie.'

'What about asking another passenger to help me?' I pleaded.

'You can't do that,' he replied. 'It is an imposition to ask for help. You must respect other people's freedom. It might inconvenience them.'

'But you want me to wear nappies,' I said. They seemed quite happy to inconvenience me.

'That is what the airline requires. They have to think of other passengers' comfort.'

'Mr Drury,' I said, 'nappies are hardly a viable solution on that score.' The whole controversy was resting on how I got to the loo. Nappies would make no difference to my need to get there. If I could change them myself I would still have to do so in the loo. Besides I had no intention of using nappies, however pressing the need, and it would be even worse for other passengers than having to help me to the loo. 'Miss Wilkie,' Mr Drury went on, 'you have to understand our situation. We are trying very hard to make things as easy as possible to put you on this flight. You are not being very co-operative, now are you?'

'Nappies and catheters are not going to make anyone's journey more comfortable. I am not paralysed. I have muscular dystrophy, which does not mean that I am paralysed from the neck down and that I have no sense of touch. It just means that I cannot walk and, in the event that I should need to go to the loo, I would only require assistance to the lavatory. As I have said before, I only weigh four stone.'

'That's fifty-six pounds for us, Miss Wilkie. Now in the event of air turbulence, fifty-six pounds is fifty-six pounds.'

'So if I wear nappies and use them, who is to change them?

'That is your problem. The crew cannot be asked to because they have to handle food.'

'But then, apart from being humiliating for me, as well as extremely uncomfortable, the passenger next to me is not going to be travelling by a rose garden.'

'I quite agree.'

'So why can't a member of the crew lift me, which is by far the simplest solution to a basically simple problem?' The conversation was now going round in circles. Mr Drury reiterated that I couldn't be lifted because of union rules. I reiterated that I only weighed four stone (fifty-six pounds to him) and that no one had ever ruptured their back on my account. He put that down to past luck and said again that I shouldn't ask to inconvenience other passengers. 'In other words,' I began, frustrated, 'you are saying that an able-bodied person is more important than a disabled one.'

'You are asking me to make a moral judgment.'

'No, I'm not,' I said. 'You have already made one.' End of conversation.

I put the phone down and rang a friend, Cherif, in tears saying I'd never been so humiliated in all my life. He immediately rang Mr Drury and tried again, first chastising him for his attitude and then trying to make some sense out of these rules. Mr Drury said nothing new, except that he now started to refer to me as 'incontinent'. My friend roundly informed him that I was not, and never have been, incontinent. Mr Drury was now embarrassed and said, 'I use the word "incontinent" because there are people around me and I do not want to offend them by using other more appropriate words relating to, you know, a delicate subject. I never for a moment wanted to suggest that she was, you know . . . um . . . incontinent.'

By now everyone was calling everyone else. The travel agent called Northwest Orient and told them to stop their nonsense and book me on the flight. Northwest Orient telexed Minneapolis to try to discover the proper wording of this ruling and I was then informed that I would only be accepted on board if I was wearing nappies. They threatened to inspect as I boarded, to make sure.

Again I pointed out that, hypothetically, I could not change the nappies by myself. 'Then you will have to take someone with you.' The only person I knew who could go was unemployed and had no money. 'We cannot make any concessions at all. The person accompanying you will have to pay the full fare.'

'I can't produce a millionaire who happens to have three weeks to spare!' At this point the woman suggested I speak to her superior, who turned out to be an echo of the Gatwick station manager.

I then discovered that the flight would have a stopover and the first leg was only seven hours long. I had been expecting a non-stop twelve-hour flight. Seven hours was not bad. I told the travel agent, Angela, that I had hung on for longer in my time and that I had flown to the Caribbean, a ten-hour flight. She conveyed this information to Northwest Orient, but they didn't want to know. I was now told that I would have to pay full price because of all the trouble I had caused.

Angela rang me back. 'I am telling you the truth now: if anything happens on the way over and you need to go to the loo they might refuse carriage on the way back. Then what would you do? Be stuck out there? Now, I perfectly understand your situation: I have a relative who is disabled. She is deaf. Now if you will permit me to make a simple analogy: she is deaf and therefore she cannot be expected to hear, now can she?'

I explained to Angela, in defiant mood, that if Northwest Orient refused to take me back I would simply get myself repatriated by the British Embassy, 'and as far as your analogy is concerned it is non-existent. I have muscular dystrophy, which in my case means I cannot walk. It does not mean I cannot travel.'

Angela tried again with Northwest Orient but every time she phoned them things got worse. They now said that they would not let me on the flight unaccompanied. Angela informed me that she had not booked me on the flight as it seemed unlikely that I was going to be able to go and she did not want to get me involved with cancellation fees. I said that I would not pay cancellation fees, I would rather go to prison. I investigated the possibility of Mobility International offering me a grant to pay for the fare of someone who would accompany me, but this was never really serious.

The phone rang again and this time it was a Mr Wheeler from Northwest Orient's reservations office in London.

'Miss Wilkie, we understand that you have been having problems over the last two weeks.' That was one way of putting it. 'I must inform you,' he went on, 'that we are unable to come to a decision before we receive a medical certificate.'

'But I sent you one two days ago.'

'Yes, I know. It's the wrong one. Your doctor will know what is needed. It must comply with C.A.A. regulations.' I had never been told that there was some kind of special form required, nor did my doctor seem to know about it, but Mr Wheeler suggested that she contact the doctor at British Caledonian Medical Centre if she had any questions. I went to Northwest Orient's office in Albemarle Street and eureka, such a form did exist. It was a rather unpleasant form which stipulated that they would not carry people with 'repulsive skin conditions'. The doctor at British Caledonian Medical Centre spoke with my own doctor and, although he was not as familiar with my case as it had been implied he would be, he just said that I should be seated next to an aisle and that there was no reason to think that I could not travel. We delivered the new medical certificate and the next day visited the travel agent's office to get news of the booking.

Now they flatly refused to take me. Northwest Orient was contacted by the agent and I demanded to speak to a Mr Snow, with whom I had previously 'communicated'. He simply told me that a decision had been made and that I could not fly. 'Who made the decision?' I asked.

'Your own doctor, the doctor at British Caledonian and the Muscular Dystrophy Group decided together that you are not fit to travel alone.' I told him that both the doctor at British Caledonian and a more senior colleague in Northwest Orient had the day before agreed that I could fly and that I only need contact them if I had any further difficulties. Mr Snow said that they both now agreed with him that I could not fly unaccompanied. I was outraged, especially at what seemed to be a conspiracy that involved the Muscular Dystrophy Group. I could not understand why they would say such a thing. I rang Mr Wheeler. He told me that they could not make a decision until they had received the medical certificate.

'But I have just spoken to Mr Snow who told me that I cannot go.'

'Yes, that's right.'

'But how can you make this decision when you have not seen the proper medical certificate from your office in Albemarle Street, which complies with your C.A.A. regulations, signed by myself and by my doctor? According to Northwest Orient's own conditions, I am perfectly fit to travel on my own.'

Their whole approach was blowing my sense of logic. I have a Classics degree and classical dialogue is a very, very logical way of arguing. You have to think back but also see ahead and carry a whole thread of logic in your mind. These people were being quite illogical.

'I'm sorry but the decision has been made.'

'But you don't have the medical certificate.'

'You can't go.'

That was their final word but it was not mine. I rang my own doctor, who was very surprised to hear of the change around. She had not spoken to anyone that morning with reference to my case and so had not retracted her opinion that I was fit to fly. I also rang the doctor at the British Caledonian Medical Centre and taped our conversation to avoid further confusion and contradiction. He told me that each airline had different rules and that 'in sober truth' most people would pick me up and would be happy to do so, but he didn't think I was going to get round Northwest Orient. He advised me that, as far as the airline was concerned, I would need to obey the letter of the law, and he pointed out the absurdity of the airline ruling in a very apt manner. 'Supposing you'd got a ninety-seven-year-old lady to accompany you who was totally incapable of raising a teacup, when you'd got into the aircraft then the cabin staff would do anything that was necessary.' However, he had continued, if I boarded the plane unaccompanied, the cabin staff would be within their rights to walk off the plane.

He said he had not spoken to anybody from Northwest Orient and had given no opinion directly to them. Neither had he been forewarned of my own doctor's call. So it seemed that the conspiracy of medical opinion to prevent me travelling did not really exist, but no one could make Northwest Orient take me.

I finally flew to the States on a last-minute cheap single to New York on Orbitrose who raised no objections at all to my presence, and picked up an internal United Airlines flight from New York. When I told them I was disabled neither airline flinched. They said that they only needed to know whether I was a) totally incapacitated, b) needed help walking, c) needed help up the stairs. I don't really come under any of those categories, but at least they were ready for me, all they needed to do was put it down on the computer. They dismissed in one sentence all I had been forced to fight over for several weeks. Our last difficulty was an unexpected hitch. It was not long after the Iranian hostage crisis and when an Egyptian friend went down to the Embassy to get my visa they would not let him in.

On June 2nd, the day I should have been flying out, I received one final call from Mr Snow. 'In view of the medical evidence the answer is absolutely, definitely NO! In the future, Miss Wilkie, do not hesitate to contact me should you need help. As you know, we do a lot for disabled people, as a matter of fact we are having a "do" for muscular dystrophy people on June 19th at Gatwick Airport. Perhaps you would care to come?' Not a lot. What a shame I'd have to miss it – I'd be in America!

Who's the Cripple, Mr Airline?

I am not blind
but you can't see

I am not deaf
but your ears are
a million times more closed
than mine

I am not dumb
but you speak nothing
intelligible

I am not epileptic
but you have fits
at the mere thought of disability

I am not paralysed
but you are more unfeeling
than a stone

I cannot walk
but you are more unmoving
than a mountain

I am weak
but my willpower is even stronger
than your fixed determination
to give me degradation
and worse treatment
than baggage

7

'With a wide open country in my
eyes and these romantic dreams in my head'
Bruce Springsteen

All the events and arguments over my flying to the
U.S.A. were very depressing. Some of the phrases and
the things that were said were all the more disturbing
because I'd heard it all seven years before when I had
struggled to stay at my Sixth Form. We had just had the
International Year of Disabled People in 1981 and yet
here were not only the same attitudes but even the same
words thrown at me.

I suppose some things had improved. Facilities such as
ramps had been placed in some municipal buildings to
make it marginally easier to get about. The Barbican Arts
Centre in London is a good example in that respect but it
is a new building. Cinemas and old theatres are more
difficult, as I found out when I wanted to see the film *A
Soldier's Story*. For the first time in my life I found myself
banned from a public building. The Classic Haymarket
informed me that because of the Greater London Council
(as it then was) fire regulations, I was not allowed in.
The manager could give me no written proof when I
demanded it. He just told me he had too many steps
and repeatedly said, 'I know how you feel.' When I
enquired about the reasons he merely walked away.

My anger at the time is summed up in a letter I wrote to
City Limits. 'What makes my blood boil is the total illogi-

cality of such people. If I had been on crutches I would have been allowed in. Yet in the event of a fire I would get out ten times as quickly as the person with crutches because I'm small and my friends pick me up and carry me all the time. Why do people have to freak as soon as they see a wheelchair?' I also wrote to my boyfriend at the time, 'The manager rang to say they only allow people in who can get out of their chair into a cinema seat and back again (and do three somersaults in the air) totally unaided. I said "Well, what do you think they're doing in the bloody chair in the first place??!"'

Fire regulations are becoming increasingly strict in old buildings. In the past they parked you in the aisle and turned a blind eye. But now the concern about safety is approaching paranoia. Even in America, when we spent a few nights in a log church, the fire marshal came to chat about the 'handicap fire regulations' and told us that we had to sleep alternately one able-bodied and one disabled person. I never knew fire officers checked up on people's sleeping arrangements but I was even more amused when I learned he had told the church that they had too many smoke detectors and too many fire extinguishers! You can't win!

That American holiday was an adventure in itself, once I actually got there after all the hassle over my ticket. It was great to be with an international set of people on the work camp. There were some from Finland, Sweden, Denmark, Trinidad, Japan and one from Bahrain where apparently the facilities for disabled people are excellent. Now we were in America all together and we were pioneering America's first integrated 'work camp' or working holiday. Disabled and able-bodied people had committed themselves to a holiday of repainting, rebuilding and scrubbing floors in order to provide better facilities for other people's holidays. I suffered the usual problems with the transatlantic language barrier: 'dustbins' are 'trash cans' and 'flannels' are 'wash cloths', so when I said my washing was drying by the dustbins it was not found for ages. But there was one word which I was surprised to hear them using and that was the word 'handicapped'. This was 1983, and Britain had long since moved on from using the word 'handicapped' to describe people with disabilities. To those of us who are disabled the word 'handicap' is like 'wog' or 'nigger', a term of abuse. I agree that it isn't quite as strong as those insults because generally the people who use words like 'nigger' are deliberately being offensive, whereas the people who say 'handicapped' think it's the correct terminology, due to ignorance. A 'handicap', to use the dictionary definition, is 'that which hampers,' i.e. it is what is imposed upon you by society, by attitudes rather than one's own disability. We are all disabled in some way, though many choose not to see it! A possible derivation of the word 'handicapped' is beggars having their 'caps in hand' and we are certainly not beggars.

That was why I was surprised to discover, on my first evening in America, that we were to watch a film entitled *Handicapped Ski Programme for Spastics*. We also did some work on a 'handicapped campsite', although I never found out whether it was I who was supposed to be 'handicapped' or the camp. In practice, however, America is more integrated than we are: it is illegal to discriminate against someone with a disability whereas the British government denies the necessity of such legislation.

Despite the apparent lack of tact in the Americans' use of this word 'handicapped' this project was their first integrated work camp for disabled and able-bodied people. I was amazed that I had actually heard of it, but then I have always been a pioneer and have consciously tried to go where other disabled people have not been. Quite accidentally, I was doing it again.

There were three venues for the work-camp and our first stop was particularly idyllic. We were in a little log cabin on the shores of a lake. The quickest form of transport was by boat and it was very quiet. The organisation was tight but I did feel that they all took themselves a bit too seriously. We had intense meetings to discuss our feelings about each other and how we were getting on. I thought that was all a bit much. I'd gone for a working holiday, I had not gone to 'find myself' through a crash course in psychotherapy. The previous work camp I'd gone to, in Ireland, had been much simpler. There were moments when I wondered whether all the effort to get on this American holiday (oops, sorry 'work-camp') had been worth it. Beautiful though the surroundings were, there were no phones and I had to rely on the office to try and chase return flights. I had, after all, only managed to book a one-way ticket out, and after an unexpected payment for a night at a hotel during the stopover, my money was limited.

Our job at that first venue was to clean up a Lost Creek 'handicapped campsite', and my task was to clean rusty old camp stoves with a wire brush. Apart from being out in the cold and drizzle (I didn't mind that) there was a good feeling among the people working together. Later, there were complaints from the able-bodied in our party who felt that some disabled members were not pulling their weight. I personally felt it was unnecessary to get up at six in the morning every day. This was supposed to be a holiday and we were meant to enjoy it and have a bit of fun. A fair amount of free time was allocated but, with the shadow of an early morning start hanging over me, it felt restricted.

The second work venue was in the mountains and was freezing cold even with seven layers of clothing. I had thought that summer in America would be warmer than in England but I wasn't thinking of mountain temperatures. Immobilised by seven layers of clothing and a hard hat to 'cap' it all, I could have been mistaken for a bundle of jumble.

One of our trips out was up Mount Hood in a snowcat, a covered tractor-like vehicle with caterpillar tyres. There was snow everywhere. It was a very bumpy ride and we had no support in the snowcat. Some of us fell on top of each other. Although it was sunny down below it was freezing on the mountain, seven thousand six hundred feet up and I got hypothermia, or so I believe. Consequently I was miserable and not at all well when we arrived at our next destination, a Jewish community called 'Shivtei Shalom', Tribes of Peace.

Things were not improving. Not only was I ill but also I was running out of money. Our last venue did not exactly provide the best facilities for getting to the loo; my room was at one end of the grounds and the loos were at the other, not too good as now I had a stomach upset.

In Oregon itself, however, the facilities for disabled people were impressive. At the time, many of the buses were equipped for disabled people and they were adapting more. One or two of the work camp people in Oregon asked me why I hadn't brought my electric wheelchair because that, combined with Oregon's facilities, would have meant I could have been much more independent. As it was, I had to be pushed and I think this may have caused some resentment. Still, I wasn't the only one.

Our last stop on the organised part of the trip was a stay with a family. Before I had booked the trip, I had been under the impression that this would mean I would integrate with an able-bodied family who would act as hosts and perhaps even show me around. My 'family' turned out to be a single woman, Kay, who was quadriplegic. She had people coming in to help her but no one had brought up the question of who would personally assist both myself and Seiyu, the other person assigned to Kay.

Seiyu was Japanese. He also had muscular dystrophy and took a fancy to me. He was not the only one to fall under the spell of my charms: another young man fell out of his wheelchair trying to kiss me. Seiyu, however, was not my type. He snored like a dying dragon and we were billeted together in the same bedroom! I don't know whether the organisers thought we would not be capable of hanky-panky because of our disabilities. It is just as embarrassing for a disabled person to be forced to share a bedroom with a person of the other sex, especially one who fancies you, as it is for an able-bodied person. Not surprisingly, this added fuel to the fire because Seiyu actually asked me to have sex with him! I don't recollect my reply, but it quenched the flames sufficiently for him to apologise and say that no sex was a good experience! What with Seiyu's snores and offers of sex it is easy to see why I did not get much sleep.

Lack of sleep did not help my anxiety over getting a flight back. I could not get hold of Marina, my travelling companion, in New York and I was so short of money that I was by now really worried. I went to the Post Office to see if I could get any money from my Girobank account in England. I was told I could not do this anywhere. That was the last straw. I came out of the Post Office with tears streaming down my face. I had fought so hard to come on this holiday and now it was proving difficult to return! I needed a large sum of money to purchase my ticket. All I could do was pray. Miraculously, a guy came up to me in the street and gave me a cheque for two hundred dollars. He wasn't worried about the return of the money, saying he knew I would get it back to him. He trusted me completely. He was like one of those angels in the Bible except he was called Eric.

However, needless to say, that wasn't quite the end of my difficulties. When I tried to cash the cheque the bank told me I had to do it at his own branch, which in turn wouldn't do anything until they had checked with Eric the Angel to ensure that it was a *bona fide* transaction and I wasn't robbing him. But one doesn't rob angels. I had to go back to Eric to get him to rewrite the cheque direct to T.W.A. so that in effect he would buy the ticket. I booked the ticket and the following afternoon the travel agent brought it round. I actually saw it in her hand. She was about to hand it over when I said my cheque was made out to T.W.A. and the ticket disappeared again. I had to do the transaction at the airport in New York, because the cheque meant that the travel agent could not collect any commission. I wrote in my journal at the time: 'Apparently it will be down in the computer so nobody else can buy it. Still it isn't very nice not having a ticket in my possession at this late stage.'

I flew out to New York to join Marina on June 26th and discovered that the travel agent had booked my ticket for the end of July, not June. If only I had been able to touch it! The friend I had hoped to stay with had gone away, I only had ten dollars and Marina had booked me into a hotel for fifty dollars a night. A few panicky phone calls and some strings pulled with a friend of a friend of Marina's in British Airways got me a ticket home on June 29th, which left me with three days before travelling train-boat-train to a wedding in Holland. I had one day to get over jet lag, one day to unpack and one day to pack again!

My journal for June 26th and 27th reads: 'Marina had booked me into the Chelsea Hotel where Dylan Thomas stayed just before he died. The room is dirty, dilapidated with peeling plaster and a filthy phone. The loo seat broke as soon as I sat on it and the bath overflowed because the taps didn't turn off. The bathroom flooded and I had to call for room service. I asked for some dry towels but was told there were none left in the whole hotel. I dried myself with the bedspread. This revealed the risky bed and I took one look at it and decided to sleep on the floor in my trusty sleeping bag (which I've spent the last three weeks doing anyway).

'Marina went out to buy some food, and when she returned she found a man had been shot in the head in the lobby. She was sick. I have a love/hate relationship with New York. I left the light on all night. I locked the door and put a chair in front of it but I still had nightmares about a murderer. In the morning I decided to draw the curtains to let the sun in but the curtains fell down, rail and all. Marina took a photo of me draped in the musty, mustard coloured curtains holding the loo seat. It was positively pleasant to get out on to the street, but that was soon spoilt by the sight of a decrepit junky, which started one thinking about the circumstances that brought him to such a state. It's a violent city.'

100

New Yorkers themselves seemed hard, rude and impatient. Even getting a cab could turn into a ridiculous saga. On one occasion it was pouring with rain and I was 'parked' in a doorway while Marina went off to hail a cab. When she finally struck lucky she said, 'I'll just go and get my friend,' but as soon as the driver saw me he was off like a flash. No one would help us trying to cross the road, even though the kerbs were far too steep. Police cars would honk at us to get moving and people were loath to help even if we asked them to. New York is not a place for disabled or decent people, it seems.

Looking back over this holiday it sounds like one long sob-story, enough to put off any sane person from travel for life. The major stress and misery stemmed from other people not coming up with the goods and should have been avoidable. But I was partly at fault for contemplating the trip through a rose-tinted imagination, but traumas are a part of life's rich tapestry and teaching. I learned to be more wary of what I'm letting myself in for. However, there were many happy fun-filled hours in Oregon such as the river-raft trip, outdoor rock concert, Jewish wedding celebrations, a paint fight and appearing on American television. I only said one sentence but people went over the top in calling me a T.V. actress star. A first taste of things to come – maybe!

Whenever you step out into the unknown you cannot pre-plan every detail. Risks are inevitable if you enjoy excitement. Sometimes you must either go for it and grab a once-in-a-lifetime opportunity or you live with regrets. Strangely it's not always difficulties but often the missed opportunity that creates unhappiness.

8

'Here I am again in this mean old town'
Dire Straits

'I've thought of living in London but unless I have an adapted flat, a job and some sort of transport, it would be out of the question.'

I wrote this to Rosie when I was still touring with Theatre of the Disabled. Further letters reveal that I was possibly planning a future London existence: I mention the first time I travelled in a London taxi by myself, clearly an important advance for me. All my friends had moved to London, and my parents had moved house when I was away on holiday in Austria in August 1982. I had arranged to go with one young man who had written me a rather wonderful love poem, but somehow on the holiday I got involved with somebody else and I wrote him a poem! He gave me a picture on which he wrote, 'To Ellen, perhaps my best memory of 1982 and certainly a part of my life . . .' When I returned, and the new contract with Graeae did not materialise, I had to give up my Aldershot flat, but after a taste of independence I did not want to go back to living with my parents. The new home was anyway unfamiliar to me. I had the growing conviction that London was where I should be.

It wasn't simply an attraction to the bright lights, job prospects and all my friends there. It was an inexplicable affinity with the place combined with a strong feeling that this was the next stage for me. I cried my eyes out for a day about the Graeae job but when the upset was thus purged from my system I announced to my parents that I was moving to London. I never verbalised, 'It is God's will' but I knew it was. I have never been so sure so soon about such a major decision in my life. That's how I was able to get over my pain so swiftly. I think my parents probably had some doubts as to the feasibility of London but they never pooh-poohed the idea to my face and never stood in my way. I had, in fact, hinted before that I would like to live in London and I was constantly dashing up to the capital to stay with friends and go to concerts or parties.

The reality of living there was a different matter and I had to be practical about sorting out a flat. I wrote to and rang all the housing associations I could think of – the length of their waiting lists was a huge shock. The John Groomes Housing Association had a waiting list of a hundred people. I gulped and wondered how often people moved out. Of course there is no regularity about it. However, the fact that I was in a wheelchair gave me some kind of priority. After a week or so of waiting I got a letter from John Groomes saying they were building a new block of flats in Hounslow – Hounslow? – and asking me if I wanted to be put on the short list. It was a difficult decision; Hounslow was hardly my idea of London and there was no way I could get transport. I would literally be stranded. But then I thought that if I said 'no' they wouldn't think I was desperate and I might lessen my chances of getting a flat where I wanted to be. I agreed to see somebody from the Association in the hope that personal contact might help my cause. It did. The director came to see me and I made my case sound as desperate as possible.

I told him how unsuitable the house in Bristol was for me now, how all my friends lived in London, in north London in fact, which was where their London block was, and I told him how depressed I was living in Bristol. It must have had some impact because within three weeks I got a letter saying that someone in the block in north London had died so there was a flat free and would I like it? Would I like it? I was over the moon. I moved in three weeks. It was an absolute miracle. I had jumped the hundred-person queue. I was exceptionally 'lucky' and I knew it and I have never forgotten.

Another 'miracle' happened when I moved in. I had to work out a way to get myself on and off the loo from my wheelchair. In Aldershot I did not use a wheelchair and elsewhere I had always had people to lift me. I had no idea whether it was physically possible, but lo and behold, I managed! I felt very pleased with myself. How I had envisaged living in a flat and relying on someone to lift me on and off the loo all the time I don't know!

I still live in the same block now, in a two-bedroomed flat on the ground floor. My first flat had only one bedroom and when I had flatmates they had to sleep in the living-room so had limited privacy, particularly as the flat was open plan. Every time I buzzed in and out to the kitchen I risked disturbing them. Eventually we rigged up a curtain, but that didn't cut out the noise of my electric chair.

Q. When is a Home Not a Home?
A: When it's Squashed Flat

So I live here too?
Thanks for reminding me
I was on the point of reminding you
No, do help yourself to my computer
Please grace it with your touch
Don't feel bad that I can't even get near it
I can buy myself another
computers don't cost very much
Sit in the most comfortable chair
put your feet up
I'd be honoured to bring you a cup of tea
and when I'm watching my favourite programme
Do flick thro' all the other channels on TV

I notice you're addicted to the filter coffee I bought
Funny, I am too
but empty the packet, feel free
I'd hate to intrude, don't mind me
I wouldn't want you to go short
You drained dry my £25-a-bottle Eau de Odour?
Oh don't mention it
how about trying on all my clothes
you and I are much the same size
so I'm sure they'd be a perfect fit
Invite all your friends round at your leisure
I'll entertain them
No, please don't thank me
It would be my absolute pleasure
I was born to serve basically

You still think I live here?
Now for once you're in the wrong
I'm just the paying guest
paying for letting my space to be dominated
by pest after pest after pest.

We had an arrangement whereby I paid the rent and my
flatmates gave me their time in return. They helped with
things like washing-up, cooking and general domestic
chores. Initially I was dependent on the social services for
any extra help. I had a home help who came twice a week
and one of those sessions was designated shopping only,
so there was a limit to how much housework she could do
in the other session.

After a while in that first flat my flatmate moved out
and I was left living on my own. I did enjoy that, but there
were dangers. They say most accidents happen in the
home and even in my flat I have to be careful, especially if
there is no one around. Due to my limited strength, I am a
bit more vulnerable and I can't always extricate myself
from awkward situations – like the night I spilled a whole
carton of cream on my kitchen floor. I told myself not to
cry over spilt milk and covered it with newspaper as best I

could, then left a trail all round the flat with my creamy wheels. Although it was exceedingly irritating it wasn't overly distressing, which is more than can be said about the day I fell out of my wheelchair.

I was actually on my own that day and I bent down to pull a plug out of a socket. This was an action I had done many times before but for some reason something went in my side and I half fell out of the left side of the chair where there is no arm rest. I didn't fall completely out because I have a velcro strap to hold me in. If I had fallen all the way out, I could have crawled to the phone and got some help. I could not undo the strap either due to the angle at which I was now dangling. Initially I wasn't too worried because I thought I could just dangle until somebody got back, probably early in the evening, but the strap was very tight and I was finding it difficult to breathe. I started to worry. What if I fainted and stopped breathing? I thought maybe I would die of asphyxiation.

By this time I was slightly tearful and started to scream for help, but nobody could hear me above all the traffic noise outside. At least I knew there was somebody coming to do some repairs late that afternoon and he was my only hope. As soon as I heard the doorbell I screamed for all my worth in the hope that he would hear me. It was by then excruciatingly painful. He eventually called through the letter box and I told him what had happened and he asked how he could get in. I replied that the caretaker had a spare key, but the caretaker had gone out so a neighbour came to the rescue. He had heard my screams before but thought the noise was kids playing when, finally, he decided to investigate. He broke the lock on the kitchen window and climbed in over the sink, which appealed to my sense of the dramatic. I was groaning by this time and the feeling of relief as I was lifted into a sitting position is indescribable. For an hour afterwards I couldn't stop shaking or crying if I tried to speak. My neighbours insisted my doctor examine me but I only had internal bruising.

Quite often accidents are caused by taking a risk, and

then one only has oneself to blame, as was the case recently. On this occasion I took a short cut. I went into my bedroom to go to bed and there were some clothes on the floor preventing me from getting close enough to the bed to transfer. I should have moved them but I thought I would risk bumping over them in the chair and 'leaping' over the gap between chair and bed. The risk backfired and I fell into bed in the wrong position, unable to turn over. Of course it would be a night my flatmate was away. I thought I could pull the duvet over me and try sleeping in that awkward position, but the more I pulled the duvet the further I slipped over the edge of the bed.

The radio was still on and I realised I could reach it. I thought, 'At least I can turn the radio off and then I might have a chance of going to sleep.' As I reached over to the radio I felt the telephone from where I lay. 'Telephone, contact outside world.' I knew if I could reach it properly I could dial for an ambulance. I thought I had remembered where push button '9' was on the dial grid but my first call simply put me through to a member of the public. I must have pressed the recall button. I realised then that I must get a look at the grid to locate push button '9'. After a long struggle I got the telephone down on to my chest, then all I had to do was lift it. This was another struggle and by this time I was trapped between my bed and the wheelchair in a very painful position.

I do not know how long it took me to discover the magic number '9'. Time loses its meaning in those situations. I was all right once I knew help was on the way. When the ambulance came they called through the letter box. Lying on my back, choking on my tears had left me with little breath to shout back, telling them who had a key and where the caretaker lived. In the end they must have woken up the caretaker and, at last, I heard the key in the lock. Once again I was rescued.

While I had been battling with the telephone, although I felt very alone, I happened to notice a poster on my wall advertising a single called 'Strength'. Later on, the Bible

107

verse came to me which said: 'I will not leave you desolate'. It occurred to me that 'desolate' means 'completely abandoned' and I had not been left completely abandoned because I had found contact with the world outside my flat via the telephone. God's promise had been fulfilled. I further philosophised and thought God's part is the promise of water in the desert or light at the end of the tunnel and our part is to exercise faith by reaching actively for rescue.

Such incidents haven't put me off living independently, though sometimes in my bleakest moments I wonder why I don't give up and let everything be done for me. I know perfectly well why: because I would lose my vitality and possibly my personality.

However, it would be true to say that I cannot manage without the help which is now available eight hours a day. People are often clueless as to what my care assistants do for me.

Basically they are my arms and legs. It was a useful exercise for me once to think of all the things for which people use their muscles in a normal day, apart from walking. Muscles are in fact used for everything from the moment you wake up. Without them you could not fling back the bedcovers, get out of bed, wash, shower, dry yourself, comb your hair, get clothes out of drawers, open the wardrobe, dress, draw the curtains, clean your teeth, squeeze the toothpaste, put the lid back on, drop it, put it back on again, open the post . . . and that's only the beginning. Muscles are used all the time and, as I have very limited muscle power, it's small wonder I am tired at the end of the day. Each one of these tasks is an effort for me, so I need more sleep but that has a knock-on effect and means my days are shorter. Thus I have to work harder in my waking hours to get everything done. That's why, as I get more successful and I am asked to do more things, often as favours, I have to say 'no' and hope that people understand that I must streamline what little time I have in the day to work. As some things get more difficult, it is also a matter of making the most of the time and care I have available to me. For instance, I can still get myself to bed, but it exhausts such a disproportionate amount of time and energy that it is an uneconomic use of my time. It's better to surrender a little independence and preserve time for more important things.

While living in London was great and the first flat was well adapted, the care system was minimal so this led to some real downers. During a period spent living on my own in my first flat I wrote to my friend Cherif: 'It's now really BUGGING me, this stupid lack of a volunteer business. I do not want to rely on friends. I feel that once I get some help sorted out I'll be more at peace in my little home, which sometimes feels more like a trap. I don't mind being alone at night, I really don't (after all, as Margueritte Yournecer says: "You're not existing for a few hours, you're in the land of the dead"). But during the day, day after day after day with no real means of escape. I really have a love/hate relationship with London . . . How can I ever explain so that other people understand what it's like to have such a lack of physical strength that you dread a simple (to others) action like having a shower (which requires no thought, strength or willpower for most human beings). Even the mere act of living can become a drag . . . I don't want to complain . . . I just feel so helpless, useless and full of frustration sometimes.'

At that time I had only written to Cherif to continue a conversation we had when he came to visit me. I had meant to ask him to do a few jobs round the flat. I wrote to Cherif again when I discovered that my French au pair Marie-Pierre, who had lived with me for four months, wanted to leave a week earlier than planned. She was in love and wanted to see her boyfriend. She had asked a friend to break the news to me because she was afraid I would still be annoyed with her after she went back to France and not want to stay with her that summer as we had planned. That in itself upset me, as she had not realised I do not hold grudges. 'It's very annoying of

Marie-Pierre,' I wrote, 'because she decided ages ago she was leaving a week early but she didn't tell me even though she knew I wanted a full month to find someone else. A week doesn't make much difference to her but for me to find a new flatmate it makes a hell of a difference. She was missing her boyfriend. I know love's the strongest pull and all that, but I wish it wouldn't make people so selfish. She has caused me unnecessary anxiety about being left stranded. I wanted to cry into someone's shoulder but I cried into the radiator instead. I had to go into the bathroom because if I cried in front of Marie-Pierre she'd feel even worse.'

As usual in these situations I blamed myself for being 'such a hassle', but having no flatmate and little domestic assistance was a dangerous situation for me. No matter how much more assertive I become as I grow older, it is still not easy to ask people to do things for me. I can never reconcile my need for people around me to be my arms and legs with my love of my own space. I'd like to rub a magic lamp and have a genie appear. Well, wouldn't we all? I have to accept a compromise.

Anyway, Cherif wrote back, 'I can see you're extremely worried. The reasons you have given me seemed relatively unfounded, i.e. you are definitely not a burden, GET THIS INTO YOUR HEAD ONCE AND FOR ALL. You never could be in a million years. Why then do you think you're so important to a lot of other people?' No matter how much I may have known this intellectually, I still needed someone to convince me verbally.

My next flatmate was a quiet-spoken young woman I got through an advert in the *Lady*. We had a good relationship but she vanished without trace one day. When I discovered she had not turned up at work either I was very concerned for her safety and notified the police. Police are not obliged to follow up an adult's failure to return home, but when I said my flatmate was a diabetic and might be in a coma they took the matter more seriously and managed to track her down. Due to a personal crisis she only returned to collect her belongings. Quite apart from my worry over her I had again to cope on my own at home. I made an emergency telephone call to Rosie, who was a social worker in London by this time, and she arranged for a district nurse to get me out of bed in the mornings, which was a good start.

Eventually I moved into a two-bedroomed flat and shared it with my friend Helena. When she left London in 1987 things came to a head. I was close to despair because even my minimal hours of work twice a week from the home help were not sacrosanct. If it wasn't a union meeting one day it was emergency calls the next. For instance she might be doing my ironing and then be summoned by her office to get an urgent pint of milk for a client and that would leave me with a pile of wrinkled clothes.

I knew I must try and get more appropriate back-up. I was fortunate to hear of the Case Manager Project (now called Choice). This is an independent advice service, a charity, which is aimed at giving disabled people more say in running their own lives. A qualified advocate called Alistair Anderson came to interview me about my individual needs and became my case manager. He compiled a package of care whereby I had two assistants, whom I chose myself, and who would work for me eight hours a day. This meant I could buy a car because part of their job would be to drive me around, rather than my having to call cabs or Dial-a-Ride. Alistair also negotiated on my behalf and persuaded the social services and the local health authority to share the cost of paying for these attendants. Why somebody able-bodied has more clout than the person who is actually disabled I don't know, but the reality is that they do. Personally designed paid help is vital because it's dependable and cannot be seen as a favour. If a disabled person has to rely on a friend or a volunteer then the guilt starts again. We are made to feel guilty for needing help and the situation can become unbearable: frustration on the one side, resentment on the other. But if they are paid the relationship is much better defined and much less strained.

The fundamental difference it has made to my life is that my care assistants now fit in with my routine; I don't have to fit in with theirs. If I need to get to work early I can ask and expect to be woken early and if I want a lie-in then I just have to say so. If I want to be driven somewhere for work or pleasure I now have my own car and a driver and the incredible freedom that brings. I can even have people round for a meal without expecting them to cook it as well. Before, it was somewhat embarrassing to invite someone, then say, 'Here are the ingredients, cook this.' At one time I employed two Sixth Formers (using my attendance allowance) to cook several dishes once a week. When they left, due to the pressure of exams etc., I put an advertisement in the local paper for part-time help on a flexible hours basis. I was inundated with replies and took on a local woman who, apart from cooking, did odd jobs like dying my hair, plus all the things home helps are not allowed to do, which includes, apparently, cleaning windows, defrosting fridges and even washing hairbrushes.

London

This beautiful, sprawling, polluted mass
a yellow-grey sky yawning
a grey time of day
the city bereft of bowlered brollied business-men
brightened here and there by a punk or three
with feather-duster and bog-brush hairdos
darkened by their top-to-toe black
in mourning for
themselves?

the East never blossoms
and like the 1940s
unchanging
never raises objections

impressive monuments
exciting for a moment

112

On the beach in Salcombe,
aged 2

'My mother stays soul
comforter always'

Family portrait, Ellen centre-stage

Above Catching bubbles

Right Learning to swim

Left On holiday in France

Alcuin, John, Pauline and Andrew 1972

Above Acting with Graeae

Left Acting with the Theatre for the Disabled

ublication of Pithy Poems 1985

Above Touring in India

Right Double Exposure

Below Publicity photo for
Equity card

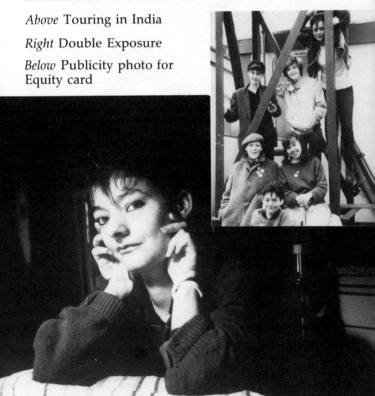

obility work camp, USA

len and Princess Michael of Kent

Presenters for Channel 4's 'Same Difference': Rudi
Breakwell, Peter White and Ellen

sink out of impression
as they become the backcloth of daily life
this city
an aunt perhaps for special visits
is no mother for our children

It may sound as though living in London and getting set up there was a full-time job in itself, but all these arrangements had to be dealt with while I was trying to establish my career in acting and later on in television. While I was looking for a flat I made a trip from Bristol to the Arts Centre Group in Waterloo. The Arts Centre Group is an organisation set up to give people who are professionally involved in the arts and who are also Christians a chance to meet, talk, eat and discuss their faith and their work. I stuck a notice up on their noticeboard when I had moved to London and soon got a flatmate. I also met Marina Green who told me that she had been thinking of setting up an integrated theatre company for able-bodied and disabled actors. She had previously set up such a company and taken a show called *Butterflies are Free* to Edinburgh. This had been about a blind man but she had been unable to find a blind actor, although she could not believe they did not exist. We decided to try and resurrect her company, 'Green Theatre Company', but such things are easier said than done.

Funding, as ever, was the main problem. We had no money so our publicity wasn't first class, but then you need publicity before you can get money. It was the perfect chicken and egg syndrome. You can't have a company of actors hanging around doing nothing when there is no money and people simply do not hand out cash until they see that you are fairly established, e.g. rehearsing a play or possessing an administrator to get the glossy publicity together and a whole expensive package that you are supposed to present to potential money men.

We did hold a few workshops through some contacts at the Royal Shakespeare Company and some more

113

workshops for children and a few summer shows and street theatre. It was a mixture of magic and farce because magic was the director's strength. There were all sorts of tricks like fire eating, ripping up phone books and card tricks. One windy day in Covent Garden was hilarious because all the cards blew about and revealed the 'magic' and my wheelchair rather bumped about on the cobbles. Another outdoor performance for children revealed our need for a stage manager. There was one wheelchair stunt where I was supposed to fly off a ramp then quickly change wheelchairs into a battered one and come back on stage, but all the kids who were watching could see the scene change going on and were yelling, 'I saw that. That's a different chair.' We also did a mad recipe sketch, but we had been so busy making props and being our own stage managers and stage carpenters that there was not sufficient time left for rehearsals. I couldn't do my Delia Smith bit properly because I was crying with laughter at the two actors with food props all over them. In the end, I could not take it seriously and was corpsing all the time. We were not the ones supposed to be laughing! It was a lot of fun, but more hard slog than financial return (as is the case with many small theatre companies) which is probably why the whole thing began to dissipate. It was time to file it under 'E' for 'experience' if not 'R' for 'relief' when I was asked to audition for a three-week tour of India with Graeae.

9

'*God is love. Is this the final message of India?*'
E. M. Forster

Monday, 21st November 1983, one a.m.: 'I'm on the plane with the old earplugs stuffed in, feeling miles away on a planet of my own. I slept on the floor for a couple of hours and got woken by a stewardess announcing, 'In one and a half hours we will be arriving in Bombay.' There was a little leap in my stomach and the excitement hit me for the first time – I mean hit me properly. Before that, I hadn't had time to myself or time to think of anything but packing . . .'

I had said 'yes' to the Graeae audition and got the part. The initial contract with the India Company was for six weeks, three weeks of rehearsal of *Casting Out* in Britain and three weeks in India. Due to the show's success, we performed in a few London venues and took it on a short tour in 1984. We were an additional company of actors: the main Graeae Company carried on in England with an existing show. Our additional, temporary director, Nigel Jamieson, took leave from Trickster Theatre Company. Trickster's performance style was very active, using acrobatics, dance, mime and magic rather than verbal communication. Nigel himself was also a clown. This meant Nigel's training and background were somewhat different from the usual Graeae director's experience. It was an interesting challenge for us all to be working together.

At first Nigel had certain fixed ideas about our limitations; his expectations of our physical ability and agility were not vast. However his prejudice and ignorance rapidly evaporated, boiled away by our skills and ingenuity. It is fair to say that Nigel's attitude was purely the product of inexperience, an inexperience shared with many able-bodied people. He soon realised that we altered our approach to acting if and when necessary. In this sense we are not extensively limited. For example, Nigel's magic tricks were simple for someone with manual dexterity. It made no difference doing them from a wheelchair. In fact a wheelchair can be a bonus on stage because it's a mobile piece of furniture.

We arrived at Bombay exhausted but excited. I think I was the only one who managed to get any kip at all. When we landed the other two 'wheelchair actors' were put in amazing cane chairs with wheels attached. The airport itself was incredible and we were forced to fight a passageway through cases, mattresses and bags. The whole floor space was covered, nothing but piles of cases as far as the eye could see.

Our problems started straight away. Tom Watt, one of our stage managers, who later played the part of Lofty in *EastEnders*, had dual nationality and was told that he needed an extra visa which he did not have. He was ordered 'straight back on the next plane,' but in fact a little bureaucracy went a long way. Once that was sorted out, we discovered our specially made prop box on wheels was badly damaged. The whole of one end had come off and was smashed in, and one side was dented and bent as if it had been dropped out of the plane. While we were waiting in the airport a kitten came up to me and adopted me. My immediate reaction was to stroke it but I told myself I did not know where it had been and I might pick up something.

After we left the airport I saw rows upon rows of shacks and hovels made out of corrugated iron, sacks, cardboard, anything. That drive from the airport was a jumble of images; people, light and shade, the bright sun of the street contrasting with the inner dark of wayside shops, signs shouting incongruity like 'Friendly Ice Cream' or 'Kwality Ice Cream', dilapidated buildings with clothes hanging out of windows, rush-hour traffic and people sleeping on the streets twenty-four hours a day. The living conditions and the poverty were difficult to handle. I had tried to prepare myself mentally for it but how can you prepare yourself mentally for something like that? A wall, a tree, a sack, a patch of shade is a home for some people. Not some, many. Many people build shelters against the walls on the pavement, yet surrounding them there may be modern skyscrapers. I wrote to Cherif, 'You can't believe some of the things you see, for instance, a modern church in the middle of decaying Indian architecture with a fun fair right beside it. My mind is brimming over with vivid pictures that my pen cannot convey quickly enough to you . . .' I wrote that when I was beside the four star hotel pool in seventy-one degrees of sunshine listening to piped Piaf. How sacrilegious and incongruous!

I found it really hard to be in luxury hotels. Down the street whole families lived on the pavement. The hotel pools were just for the tourists and I couldn't help thinking that people were drinking water far less clean than the water other people were swimming in. I later continued to Cherif, 'I've just got back from my first trip on foot, as it were, in Bombay. I tried to buy some postcards but they just don't sell them!! It's very difficult to get time to myself to write. There are so many demands. If it's not a performance or the company it's journalists, audience, people we meet. If only I had more TIME in this crazy place . . . this is the most amazing country I've been to.'

When we arrived at the hotel, despite the fantastic garlands-and-Coke reception we were told that there weren't enough rooms for us. 'This bodes well,' we thought. I was one of the lucky ones and had been allocated a room even if there was only one bed between two of us. At least it was a double, some only got singles.

But I was optimistic if I thought a bed was the only requirement for sleep. I tried for a couple of hours but the continuous noise of car horns prohibited such a luxury. After lunch and a press conference we had to go straight to the theatre for a technical run-through, to get sound and lighting right. It took hours and we were all falling asleep but we had to do it because lovely India had, without telling us, removed Thursday's performance to Tuesday, the next day. We were horrified. We had only just arrived, and would get little sleep before the required performance. Faced with such a *fait accompli*, fed up though we were, we compromised, saying that there was no way we could do it before 11 a.m. Actors feel committed to shows. As we left the theatre, we saw a sign: 'REGRET November 22nd Performance at 11 a.m.' We did not regret it at all.

For dinner, the hotel tried palming us off with hamburgers and chips! We ordered, indeed demanded, curry. It took an hour to arrive and it was cold. I got to bed at one a.m. So much for getting over jetlag.

Generally audiences were very large which was not surprising. After all we had been billed as 'The only company of disabled actors in the world'. We first saw that advertisement on the bus which picked us up from the airport. We were booked to do four main performances, two in Bombay and one each in Calcutta and Delhi. The auditoriums turned out to be very large, but we ended up doing quite a few mini performances too. These were on our schedule as 'workshops', but in fact we mostly performed again due to the language barrier.

We did workshops for the Spastics Society of India – one in each of the three cities – which were in special schools. Sometimes the pupils acted for us too. In Delhi there was one boy who asked very intelligent questions. When he directly enquired, 'Is there better care for spastics in England and America?' it was agony to answer in such a public setting. However, this was a vast improvement on our first experience of an Indian workshop. This was in Bombay, at the Fellowship of the Physically

Handicapped, where we discovered their idea was to sit round a very long committee-type table with piles of papers in front of them. The participants would read their pompous-sounding papers and pontificate on what they might do in the future for disabled people. Our idea of a workshop was to get rid of the tables and all sit round in a circle for a start, then do workshop games involving disabled people who wanted to act, not spout. At that venue we were treated to a mini dance performance by some disabled children.

We did a proper workshop using voice exercises with some university drama students in Calcutta and they played us music and sang in return. It was typical of the Indian generosity to give in return. We were there as the entertainers and we were not expecting to be entertained. Moreover they showered us with gifts. If it wasn't sweet-smelling garlands thrown round our necks at the airports (we flew between cities), it was huge bouquets and baskets of flowers at our performances. Even at the workshop venues we were given samosas, candles or packets of Christmas cards. We rarely went away without some sort of gift. When we flew to Delhi, a blind man brought us a poem and a red rose each at the airport, which was very touching. Even so, Indian generosity can be slightly excessive sometimes, as I discovered when we were taken to have breakfast with the mayor of Bombay. Unfortunately I don't drink tea, which is an Indian national drink, so I asked for some fruit juice. What I got was some sort of strawberry flavoured milk. I don't drink milk either, particularly pink milk, and the glass was huge. I felt terrible because I had especially asked for something different and I still couldn't drink it.

At our technical run-through in Calcutta the minister of culture gave us each a bronze bowl, even though he had no interest in us or the show and walked out after ten minutes.

On November 28th, I sent a postcard to Cherif: 'I'm writing this waiting for my *alu ghobi* and *nan* to arrive . . . gosh, this land of heat and dust; I keep washing my hands but my fingernails are black the whole time. I'm the only person who hasn't been ill yet – yes, amazing isn't it? – despite the spices. Nigel voted me "Super cool cat of Graeae 1983".' I spoke too soon. The next day I was ill and Nigel changed his tune too. He said he'd never known anyone perform in such a dire condition.

On November 30th we flew to Delhi and spent our first night in a horrible hotel. It seems almost wicked to be derogatory about an Indian hotel when so many Indians live in degradation. However we were there to work, not as affluent, gawping tourists. I couldn't plug my wheelchair battery in to charge it because the plugs were wrong. Although I bought a proper adaptor, their socket would not take anything I had. Added to this, the flush didn't work, the lift had broken down, the food was dire and there was an awful band playing in the restaurant. I lost my appetite.

The following day we were booked in for tea with the British High Commissioner under the auspices of the British Council. We took the opportunity to 'mention casually' the impracticalities of our hotel and the very same day we were moved to a pleasant guest house. I went straight to bed but a party was in full swing, so the noise prevented sleep again.

In Delhi we met Mrs Indira Gandhi, then Prime Minister of India. We were performing in a vast theatre, with Mrs Gandhi in the front row. We had no idea she was coming until the day of the performance. She was apparently going to leave in the interval to attend her next appointment. The Prime Minister's presence meant our rehearsal time was interrupted by a hovering group of bodyguards testing our set and props to see if we intended to blow up the Prime Minister. The chief guard picked up a piece of wood with a nail in it and said, 'What's this?' We could only reply, 'A piece of wood with a nail in it!'

The officials began to get in the way and their pernickety checking was wearing down Nigel's normally never-ending patience. He started saying things like, 'Right, have you finished now? Can we get on?'

We were told that if Mrs Gandhi liked the show she would stay for the second half and delay her next appointment, and she did! What's more there was a standing ovation which is exceptionally rare in India. Two of Mrs Gandhi's bodyguards came on stage during the interval to inform us that she wanted to see the second half of the show and could we go on again in five minutes instead of our allotted fifteen? We were later told she never cancelled appointments but had been so impressed she had postponed her next engagement in order to stay. After the performance she came up on stage and shook hands with us all. Again we were showered with gifts of garlands and records and also taken to dinner in an expensive restaurant. Unfortunately I was too ill to be sociable and had to leave dinner early after a tiny bit of rice and yoghurt which was my first attempt at eating that day. The arts critic from *The Times of India* told me I was a superb actor so I suppose I can't have let the side down too badly.

Our hosts were so bowled over by our performance that they treated us like VIPs and wanted us to move into the Ashok Hotel where Mrs Thatcher and her delegation had just stayed for a conference. So we moved again. The hotel was very posh, with red carpeted ramps, corridors of marvellous shops and many restaurants serving different types of Indian cuisine. The rooms were beautiful, with television, radio, fridges, lovely furniture. Even the bathroom had a loo which flushed. Being ill I could not take advantage of all the luxuries on offer but it was good not to be ill in a grotty place. When a doctor came and gave me some medicine I was too ill even to take it. I didn't eat for about four days so was rapidly losing weight which I cannot afford to do. Thus the great achievement recorded in my diary: 'I ate three-quarters of a banana (with difficulty)' and my comment, 'I wish I could be fed intravenously with banana' followed by, 'Late at night I felt better and ate a tangerine'. When I finally did start to eat a bit more the first thing I fancied was boiled potatoes. Potatoes had almost always been my favourite food as a little girl. We phoned the kitchen in the Ashok and asked for a plate of boiled potatoes. Even though they were not on the menu, the man said, 'Certainly, Madam,' and came up with a whole silver tureen of boiled potatoes on a trolley. I could have been the Queen or even Maggie herself.

We didn't have much time for sight-seeing. I believe we had been allocated two token half days in three weeks. We had been given a very tightly packed schedule and with endless teas and breakfasts and meetings. The organisers thought we wanted to meet all sorts of officials but we wanted to see and absorb India. We managed a visit to the Presidential and Parliament buildings in Delhi and the Red Fort, and two days before we flew back we went to Agra for the day to see the Taj Mahal. We got up at five o'clock in the morning and went to Agra on the train. The platform was a mass of supine grey bundles. I was still very weak so slept with my head on Nigel's lap during the journey. Nigel and I took a tonga, or horse-drawn cart, to the Taj from the station. Fifty men had surrounded us and haggled over the tonga prices. Indian traffic really takes the biscuit. We passed eleven children on one rickshaw and five on a bicycle.

When I first saw the Taj Mahal through the archway I thought it was quite wonderful. Nigel had seen it before and did offer to stay behind with me if I was too ill to make it, but I said, 'No way'. I was going to see it, otherwise I would regret it for the rest of my life. Seen from a distance it is pretty wide. The view over the river behind the mausoleum, where the cows graze and bathe, is quite special. It is a part of the beauty of the Taj that is not often shown in the tourist brochures. I later slept on the grass outside the Taj Mahal. It was a peaceful paradise away from the rush of India, and green parrots flew above our heads.

When we arrived back at the station we met a man who had seen us perform in Delhi, and he told us, 'I can never give you as much as you have given me.' Knowing the extent of Indian generosity by then, I doubted it very much. I told one man I was from Mars because by then I was fed up with the incessant 'Where are you from?' As ever, in Agra we were followed by a stream of children, so it was impossible to stop and buy anything. If we stopped, a dense crowd gathered and it was a fight to break through. I called them our disciples and once counted fifty of them.

The Mogul Gardens was another bit of sightseeing we organised ourselves. A guard stopped us and said that the gardens weren't open until January, but we had seen him let other people in and when we asked why they were allowed in, he let us through. Then we came up against one of the presidential bodyguards who said they were not open until February, but when we took a photo of him and told him we were staying at the Ashok and the Prime Minister had seen us, he said he would ring reception and see us the following afternoon.

Apart from sightseeing we also had to deal with the press. One radio reporter barged into our dressing room in the interval, which is not done! But the press liked the show and their reviews reflected this, although they were not always flattering. One reviewer, Gayatri Sinha, wrote, 'To see five handicapped people on stage tell their individual and collective story of endeavour is drama of the flesh and blood. Their performance cannot but evoke your admiration when a group of several handicapped people gustily sing, "We ain't gonna beg, we ain't gonna hide. We're together to regain our pride".'

Another reviewer wrote, 'Ellen Wilkie had the pair of expressive eyes, but she had to fight a lot for her deformity which stood in the way of her becoming an actress.' The same reviewer called Graeae 'a theatre of the crippled and the deformed' but he liked us. A journalist came and interviewed me by the pool of the Ashok Hotel and asked me why I didn't go to a special school. Also, did I have a boyfriend and what was the greatest disability? She then proceeded to tell me that I couldn't travel alone or get married and have kids and asked personal questions about all the others in the company. Needless to say I did not feel it appropriate to answer all the questions, although I did set her straight on my sexual prowess and travelling ability.

The day before we returned to England we were filmed for television. The studio was tiny and the crude cameras were used badly, so goodness knows how that turned out. With only half a day left, Nigel and I went souvenir shopping, which was great fun because Nigel knows India well and encouraged me to bargain. He also delighted shop-keepers with his magic ball tricks and teased them saying, 'I bet you couldn't balance it on your nose.' Intrigued, they replied, 'Show again.' When street-vendors cried to us to buy their wares he retorted, 'It's too nice. I wouldn't want to take it away from you.' Our journey back to the hotel was my first and last experience of a trishaw. The driver was charming and on our arrival said he was, 'Very, very sorry for bumpy'.

It was when I stepped outside the hotel that I became acutely aware and embarrassed about the relatively large amount of money I was carrying. I wrote in my diary that I wanted to give it all away but it was impossible and I made a note never to go out again with so many rupees. It was thoughtless not to have emptied my purse earlier.

At Calcutta airport a large group of porters walked behind my wheelchair. Their eyes followed the joystick, not me, with absolute fascination. They do not have electric wheelchairs in India so do not understand you cannot push them. Mind you, even some English people are still ignorant and try to push my electric chair. In Calcutta market, where I stopped to buy some material, the men crowded round and asked, 'Dynamo? Battery?' One of the Spastics Society school teachers asked me where I got my wheelchair and I had to reply that I got it from the government, and that made me feel awkward. When it comes to disabled people and equipment, we may not have the best State provision but at least a government wheelchair is the norm in Britain. It can easily be taken for granted. A wheelchair like mine could have made all the difference to some people who were reduced to begging on the street. The nearest I saw to an outdoor wheelchair in India was a disabled man on a makeshift skateboard in the middle of a busy road.

I think the waste in Britain struck me more than the poverty in India because Indian people still seemed to be less marred by their poverty than we are by our materialism. That is not to ennoble poverty. Seeing cows, dogs and children eating together from rubbish dumps is anything but picturesque. One day in Calcutta, at different times, I saw people drinking from and washing themselves in the gutter, and if that is not sufficiently shocking I saw the gutter used as a lavatory too.

Strangely enough, Calcutta was my favourite of the cities where we performed. It was more lively and very verdant. Sometimes the roads were more than I could cope with: the traffic was suicidal. I witnessed a man pulling forty tea chests through three rows of rickshaws, buses, bikes, cattle trucks, taxis, cars, carts and cows. There was a man on a bus hanging on to the spare tyre. Horns were non-stop, warning, 'Get out of the way. I'm coming'. I closed my eyes as our driver almost collided with traffic coming headlong towards us, then swerved at the last minute.

I may not have been exactly at ease in Calcutta traffic, but I felt very uncomfortable being at the Country Club where we were kindly taken and served tea, sandwiches and chocolate cake.

Delhi was a startling contrast to both Bombay and Calcutta, and I always think of it as sanitised India. It didn't have the same feel to it as the rest of my 'India experiences'. With its wide open spaces, no hooters, no one in the streets, much verdure, parks and walled gardens it seemed all rather English. People were riding their bicycles very sedately and there was no one in the parks. It was as if all the beggars had been swept aside. I somehow couldn't cope with the sudden change. I did see an elephant in the road, which was not at all English, and we came across shanty towns and hovels eventually. Of course old Delhi, which is separate from new Delhi, has as much hustle and bustle as other Indian towns. The traffic was eight to ten lanes wide in tiny narrow streets and the market smelled of urine.

Obviously the begging was upsetting. The first beggar I saw was a man with a wooden leg who was asking for food outside our van. I wrote in my diary, 'Terrible, I had no money near me!' The next day there was a beggar boy outside our bus. We gave him some food and he was happy; he didn't ask for more. He begged with his eyes, which spoke volumes. I had always been aware of Third World poverty, though coming up against the enormity and extent of it was a shock. Even so, I did have more of a problem adjusting when I got back.

It did not occur to me to prepare myself for my return to England. It took a while to become accustomed to the space we have, and I kept wondering where all the people had gone. It didn't take me so long to adjust to India. Having said that, my experience of the country was a privileged and unusual one in that I was paid to work there and was not experiencing deprivations, except maybe when I was ill! Simply slotting back into everyday living in Britain took me about a week and I am an adaptable person. I actually loved India and want very much to go back and experience it as a non-working person. I wrote to Nic, 'I'll be heartbroken to leave India. I love working here and it's a very happy company. We all feel we could quite easily tour together for a year!' There was also a feeling that I ought not to like the country due to the poverty. People who live in deprivation day in, day out can still retain their dignity, and that I admire. I was reminded of a quote from a leaflet we were handed at our first workshop: 'We have never been an unkind people. But somehow in India, those tremendous survival pressures seem to make us turn a blind eye to suffering and poverty. Occasionally, a twinge of guilt prompts us to offer alms and charity to the maimed or diseased beggar on the street. Walking away, we console ourselves that

126

our burden has been lifted. But a man or a child with just one arm, a double amputee, does not need charity. Charity breeds a certain indifference. Charity only pushes their problem to a safe dark corner. What they need is an opportunity to live in dignity, to make a worthwhile contribution to the world about them, to feel that they too make a difference.'

India has a fascination, magic and moving charm which goes beyond any chocolate box picture of the Taj.

10

'Nothing worth having comes without some kind of fight'
Bruce Cockburn

A few days before I appeared in the television film *Raspberry Ripple*, a friend told me how lucky I was to be in it. The friend predicted that I would be invited on all the chat shows and inundated with offers. All I got were two agencies wanting to borrow my video for their own purposes. For my pains, one video was chewed up by the neighbour's dog when the courier put it through the wrong door. Since I've been on television I find many people younger than myself say things like, 'Oh, you're really lucky, you've made it, you're a T.V. presenter, you're famous, you're a film star.' So let's get this straight – I have been in one film, I am not a film star. Lots of people have been in films, it is no big deal. There is drama on the television every day of the week. Famous people can rest on their laurels. As a woman with a disability I am never going to be able to rest on my laurels. I will always have to strive to stay where I am.

I'd Rather be 'Able-bodied'

famous and brave are the medals I earn
cold comfort for the strength I lack
the glory for which I really yearn
is more than a patronising pat on the back
I'd rather be able-bodied than famous or brave

I won't get the exciting votes I seek
I'm typecast to play the 'physically weak'
I'm quite content with me as me
but if I'm a star through my disability
I'd rather be 'able-bodied' than famous or brave.

A crown sits awkwardly upon my head
I deserve no such honour as yet
not until I break the mould
will I win the right trophy for me to hold
'cos I'd rather be 'able-bodied' than famous or brave

press and radio may rush to my side
but the fame burns a hole deep inside
disabled is the word on public lips
can I ever escape from its clamping grips?
who'd not rather be 'able-bodied' than famous or brave?

I have wanted to say to people who envy me, like an old grandmother, 'Look, Sonny Jim, when I was your age I was earning a pittance doing fringe theatre and being unemployed. I had to serve my apprenticeship like anybody else and I've had to fight every inch of the way.' I had to struggle for years before I finally got my Equity card, for instance, when other people got theirs straight away. When I joined Graeae it was not an Equity company and I had to wait, but others joined it when it had become an Equity company and, like magic, there was their Equity card. It also took a very long time for me to get an agent. It was a few months after the second series of *Same Difference*, which I presented on Channel 4, that I got one. I had written off to various agents and phoned up, hoping someone would take me on, and remember one very snooty woman who simply said, 'I'm not taking anyone on at the moment unless they're very different. Who are you, anyway?' Well, I'd have said that I was different.

I do have to admit that both my work on *Same Difference* and my work on the film were as a result of telephone calls that came out of the blue. Freelancing, as any freelance will tell you, is a matter of writing letters, following up contacts, making phone calls and listening to 'Don't call us, we'll call you'. Invariably something comes up from a completely unexplored area, which makes you wonder why you made all those other phone calls in the first place. So it was with *Raspberry Ripple*.

The phone rang one day and it was somebody from the B.B.C. wanting to check my availability over the next few weeks. I had never been asked what my availability was, so I asked 'Availability for what?' They said they were doing a film with a lot of disabled actors. Would I be interested? I said, cool as a cucumber, 'Send me the script and I'll let you know.'

They sent me the script but they hadn't said I was up for any specific part. After I expressed my interest, they rang again and said the director was very keen to meet me. I went into the B.B.C. for a first interview and was asked which part I would like to play. Jan was the only suitable part as she was the only character who was my age, my sex and in a wheelchair. Jan was a major support role. She was the best buddy of Rick, the lead male, who was played by John Gordon Sinclair. The other parts for female disabled characters were all smaller but I was going for gold. Apparently I was up for the part of Jan anyway. It was just their way of seeing whether I would suit the character, to find out if I actually wanted to do it. Somebody told me later that the director had always wanted me for the part, but I had another two weeks to go before I found that out for myself. I remember when he looked at my Curriculum Vitae he was very impressed that I had managed to keep in work almost all the time – quite an achievement for any actress.

They called me back for a second interview, and now we were getting down to practicalities. How fast did my wheelchair go? Well, the legal limit is four miles per hour but the D.H.S.S. tamper with wheelchairs so that they can only go at two miles per hour. They can't have cripples going fast, can they? Thanks to the Manpower

Services Commission, though, I'd been provided with a 'Zippy' model since Graeae days – the D.H.S.S. one had been useless for choreography and movement about the stage. Four miles per hour was almost acceptable for the more exciting bits of *Raspberry Ripple* such as the 'heist' which involved several wheelchairs charging down the corridor of the fictitious institution. At this interview I was asked about the help I needed and I was completely honest about it. I explained that on Graeae tours the stage managers were employed not only to do the usual stage managing job, but also to help the actors during rehearsals and on tour. There are, of course, hundreds of people on a film set but they all have a specific job to do and I was bit worried that one of the specific omissions would be me. I explained in detail what help I would need on location although I could cope perfectly well in an adapted environment. I am not 'handicapped' at home. I was anxious right from the start, although at the interview I was reassured that everything would be fine.

It was Easter time and I went with my friend, Helena, to her parents' farmhouse in Devon. When we arrived, Helena's mum was on the doorstep. 'Your fame has gone before you,' she called. 'The B.B.C. have rung and they are going to ring again!' It was to tell me I had got the part. Immediately I asked about help and facilities. 'Oh, don't worry,' they said, 'that's all in hand.'

I had never been on a film set before and there were certain rules that I knew nothing about. For instance, when you get a filming schedule you are not supposed to plan anything for the days marked off. Needless to say, I did. I suddenly found myself double booked, only to be told that 'days off' are movable feasts and that you are obliged not to make any solid arrangements during the entire filming period.

People invariably say to me, 'But it was exciting filming, wasn't it?' I have to disillusion them with, 'No, it's not exciting filming. It's a job. There is a lot of hanging around and people are people the world over. They are not wildly dynamic or extra special merely because they are film actors.' People have no idea how long we sit waiting to be called, needed on set but not actually doing anything. Once I got into costume, went through make-up and waited an hour, only to be told, 'We won't get to your bit today. Come back tomorrow.'

I had never realised how many times one simple scene had to be shot before they got what they wanted from enough angles with the right emphasis. I remember the dreaded breakfast scene which even the director put off shooting and which took all day. We had to do this scene over fried eggs and bacon, which is not my favourite food at the best of times, but at least in real life you don't have it served up over and over again – *ad nauseam*. Each time the scene was shot the food had to be rearranged or recooked. It was foul. They used ninety-six eggs that day, merely as props, not to feed us, which seemed a criminal waste after what I had seen in India. At tea time I turned down any offers of food and just fell asleep at the table, I was so tired.

My all-night marathon took the biscuit, though. We were all falling asleep all over the place, and along came the floor manager shoving newly written scripts, diagrams and reorganised schedules into our hands. I had been hanging around for hours so it really did add insult to injury to alter things yet again – so much for the glamour.

I also learnt fairly quickly in rehearsals that facial expressions had to be played down much more than in theatre. Our first day read-through of the script was probably the shortest honeymoon period of any job on record. I went away feeling exhilarated by the read-through, excited at the prospect of the work ahead and confident I could do it. The next day the director took me aside and said, 'I don't know what we are going to do about your face.' He meant of course that acting for the camera is a much more intimate form of the craft and I had to learn it. It came as something of a shock to someone who had had audiences raving over her facial expressions throughout her career with Graeae. I suppose I had put all my physical acting into my face because I could not do so much with my body.

Learning on the job was by no means the major part of my problems. The trouble started almost on the first day when I realised I was not going to be getting any help, despite the fact that I had emphasised my need of it. No arrangements had been made for me. It was just like my Sixth Form experiences and flight to America all over again. These things are simple for able-bodied people to solve with a little forethought and organisation, but there had been none. I don't know whether A thought B was doing it and vice versa but the result for me was the same. I reached the point where I could not carry on.

One of the problems was that all the other disabled actors on the set were stronger than I was. Paraplegics develop very strong arms so they can do almost everything for themselves, except walk. My disability is lack of strength. Because of the strength and independence of the other actors I was on my own, fighting my own battle. Everybody in the world is uniquely disabled and many need co-operation from others to help them live their lives, some of us more than others.

We were away filming on location and no arrangements had been made for me to stay anywhere suitable. I tried to find the person responsible but because I was always rehearsing it was difficult. I could never pin down whoever was supposed to be doing it. In the end, I'm afraid I had to throw a wobbly. Luckily I had not yet signed the contract, due to the usual bureaucratic speed of the B.B.C. I told them I was not signing it or going on with the show until things were sorted out. I was in tears of course, desperately upset that I had been forced to make such a fuss, but I simply could not function on location without the proper help and I had told them so right from the start. I wanted the job very much and I wanted to do what was required of me but I did need some help to cater for my needs. It's a constant dilemma; to what extent do I state my needs and risk losing the job in the first place? And to what extent do I hold back until they take me, risking losing the job later when they say, 'Ah you never told us you couldn't do that on your own.' People had started to say things to me like, 'Haven't you got a minder? What do you do when you go on an outing?' Outing?! I wasn't a child begging to be taken to the zoo. They looked disapproving when I said I didn't have a full-time helper – chance would be a fine thing.

My wobbly worked. The director had arrived on the scene by this time and he was very understanding. He could see I was in genuine distress.

First of all they arranged to let me stay in the residents' home where they were filming. I was told I could not stay in a hotel because they could not afford it. Unfortunately the residents' home was useless. Everything was too high for me. It was higher than it was in a normal flat. I couldn't reach any of the alarm bells or door phones. Not only that, there was noise going on until three o'clock in the morning and at six o'clock a radio next door blared out its morning call. I decided that since the location was only a few miles up the A40 it would be easier to commute from London by taxi. I would lose less sleep through early mornings and late nights than by the noise of the residents' home. This was arranged, but of course booking my taxi was not always a priority and when I was leaving the set sometimes I was forgotten. I must admit that once I got so annoyed by this I stormed up to the crew saying, 'I may not be a star but I am a human being.' Admittedly, this was not a brilliant witness for the Christian faith but it illustrates one aspect of filming that made me angry at the time.

I know that a 'star' or stars are necessary to a film and I accept that they get their own caravan and a lot of attention because of what their reputation brings to a film. But if the budget is so over-stretched by employing the star that other members of the cast cannot have what they need, or are exploited, perhaps the film should not be made or made with a cheaper cast. In the end I was given a helper, who was a friend of the man who had the original idea for the film, but she was paid pocket money for working on the set when Faye Dunaway (who was playing the lead role) was provided with the most expensive stockings (fifteen pounds' worth) which she only ever wore once.

People always ask me what Faye Dunaway was like but she spoke to me only twice, once to say, 'Are you having fun?' and once to find out who my character was, although I believe she did sign my birthday card. (I had my birthday while they were filming and, although I hadn't told anybody, a cake and a card appeared which was great fun.) A signature on a card hardly means I can claim an intimate knowledge of Faye Dunaway's character. That's the way filming is. Even two of the three scenes I had with her I did not act with her. In one scene they shot her lines separately, and another they changed completely because she was not there. As with any mysterious star there were apocryphal stories spread about her and I don't know whether they were true. The best one was about the time she went out for a walk on Brighton pier and she had to wear flat shoes because heels would get stuck in the slats. She had a scarf over her head to keep her hair in place and a couple passing by said, 'Oooh look, there's Sue Pollard.' I think she went straight back to the caravan and redid her make-up.

Brighton turned out to be a good location, and a significant time for me. *Raspberry Ripple* is Cockney rhyming slang for 'cripple', hence the title of the film. There is a short dialogue in the film between Rick, played by John Gordon Sinclair, and a woman from the council who visits him. She asks him, 'What's the best thing about being disabled?' and he replies that people buy you a lot of ice cream. She then says, 'So it's better being disabled in the summer then?' or words to that effect. The punch line is Rick's: 'Yes, my favourite is Raspberry Ripple.' One day the crew were down on Brighton beach filming and I had a morning to myself, so I went for a wander along the promenade. It was a lovely day and I sat there on my own watching the crew working in the distance

135

and enjoying the sun when all of a sudden a total stranger came up to me and shoved a large melting ice cream into my hand. There was far too much of it and I didn't want an ice cream anyway. If I had wanted one I would have bought one. However, it would have been ungrateful to throw it away and, as usual, I'm sure the gentleman meant well so I waded through it as it dripped its sweet and sticky path down my fingers. All I could do was laugh, really. The man was blithely unaware of the relevance of his action to the film and the rest of the cast roared with laughter when I got back and told them the story.

In the same way as people think your career is secure once you have landed a film part, many do not realise how long a gap there is between making a film and actually seeing it on television. We filmed *Raspberry Ripple* in the summer of 1986 and it was first transmitted at Easter 1988. Even if I was to be deluged with a stream of offers, I still had nearly eighteen months to wait before the film was shown. Even then not everybody would like it.

Reviews are always amusing even when damning. Philip Purser of the *Daily Mail* certainly didn't like *Raspberry Ripple*. He found the programme silly because it depicted a disabled man longing to get out of institutionalised surroundings that Philip Purser thought were more than adequate. In other words, the disabled hero Rick should be grateful he is allowed to live in a centrally heated prison instead of being out there mixing in with the world. 'If John boy didn't like it,' he wrote, presumably meaning John Gordon Sinclair's character Rick, 'no one was compelling him to stay. There is always a waiting list of those who would give their eye teeth for a vacancy.' His review completely missed the point, which makes me wonder if he was giving the programme his full attention. The *Independent* and others gave more thoughtful accounts. Even I got a name check, '. . . a gifted documentary director looks to have a lot to offer drama. With Sinclair, Shaban and the newcomer Ellie

Wilkie all out-acting an uneasy Dunaway, *Raspberry Ripple* was a strong oddity.'

Anyway, transmission came and went and I missed the press launch because they forgot to invite me until I was already committed to filming that day for T.V.S. Despite the predictions of all those who thought that I now had it made, I got nothing from the film at all, no follow-up whatsoever. It was just as well I wasn't expecting anything. One reaction was unfortunately not a welcome one. The *News of the World* rang the B.B.C. wanting to speak to the 'girl who had fallen in love with John Gordon Sinclair'. Well, needless to say, it was the character Jan who fell in love with John's character Rick. I heard warning bells and told the woman at the B.B.C. who rang me up about it that I did not want to speak to the newspaper. She agreed, saying she would give the journalist some excuse. Half an hour later my phone rang and it was the *News of the World* journalist wanting the interview. I said, 'But I have already said that I am not going to do an interview.'

'Oh,' he said. 'Why's that?'

'Because you're a sexist, fascist paper, that's why.' (In for a penny, in for a pound.) He was a bit taken aback by the strength of my reaction but he was not put off, he just carried on blithely. 'I'm nothing to do with that side of things, I'm an arts reporter on the arts page'; but I was still not convinced. I had seen their article on Nabil (not that I bought a copy myself, you understand) and it was hardly sensitive. They had used words like 'crippled dwarf' so I told the reporter I was tired of being misrepresented and misquoted. I said that I thought they were not a trustworthy paper. He said, 'Oh, we wouldn't do anything you wouldn't like. In fact,' he went on, 'I recently did a report about someone with a disability.' I knew then that he had been responsible for the article on Nabil and that clinched it. I told him 'no' but he still tried it on. This time he told me how interesting it would be for me to meet him, 'for it's not every day you get to meet a reporter for the *News of the World*.' Was this tempting offer one I could refuse? In the end, after various verbal promises related to his integrity, he said he would ring back when I had given the matter some thought. I did give it some thought once more and spoke with my friend and journalistic mentor, Martin Wroe, himself a freelance journalist. Sadly for journalism, he told me that even if I got guarantees to see the text and change it after it had been written, they could still change it if they wanted to alter it to their editorial line. He reminded me that I would have to live with any consequences. He also speculated, as I had too, that the headline could be something like 'Kinky Cripple has Affair with John Gordon Sinclair'. I could sue of course, but who would notice? I had nothing to gain from it. I took Martin's advice and when the journalist rang back I was out and the answer was 'no'. Even then I lived in fear and dread for a week that an article would be written from our telephone conversation.

A touching finale which was more pleasant than any muck-raking journalist's offer to me was the request for my autograph from some neighbours' children.

By the time the film came out I was well into my career as a television presenter and it all seemed very distant. It was very amusing to be recognised by a fellow-holiday-maker on a Greek island. No sooner had I got off the coach for a breather at a café than 'I know you' came from a nearby table. No escape for the wicked, I guess . . . Looking back, I learned a good deal about filming, so much so that I would love to have another crack at it. Now I know all about altered schedules, long waits, late nights and the technicalities of the craft, I would have much more confidence and consequently much more fun. Plus I have my so-called, coveted minder so that side of things would be taken care of now. I hope I would do a better job too, because many is the time when I wish I had said to the director, 'Can I do that one more time please?' just to go for the better shot. I was too familiar with performing live on stage to get my mind round recordings and retakes but it was all excellent experience.

It's probably also true to say that I didn't enjoy things

as much as I might have done because the whole period was overshadowed by my relationship with my boyfriend, which at that stage was very rocky. Everything in my diary reveals that I was far more concerned about what was going on inside the world of his mind than in my world of work. I wrote virtually nothing about the shooting. Obviously the film had paled into insignificance because I was going through a real-life drama.

11

'When you're lovers in a dangerous time
Sometimes you're made to feel as if your love's a crime'
Bruce Cockburn

'These words of Bruce Cockburn's suddenly hit me as I heard them the other day for the hundredth time, and became relevant,' I wrote to Dorian at a time when our relationship seemed to be under attack from all sides. Dorian was the greatest love of my life but he was by no means the first. When I was sweet sixteen, or at least sixteen if not that sweet, I thought that falling in love was a mutual occurrence. My naivety told me it was simply a matter of time. The object of my affection would eventually succumb to the intensity of my passion, but my passion was so fiery that my dreamboat was more likely to be smothered by the heat. I had a romantic idea of my knight in shining armour sweeping me off my feet, but soon a cold grey realisation dawned that this is not the stuff of life itself. It took years to dawn on me, though. I was wise enough not to tell my first love, Sam, my true feelings. I think he would have been too sensitive to take it. I was not so wise the second time round, in my student days, and lived with regret when I saw our friendship soured. I learned never to admit being in love to a man again.

At sixteen, I also had to deal with the competition. I was not the only one to fall prey to the charms of the good-looking Sam, which caused some problems. 'I can't speak about Sam at the moment as it is rather a sore subject and I am afraid I might cry. I'll talk about the dear boy when I continue my letter,' I wrote to Rosie, the only person I could tell about the matter. 'I'm not on desperately good terms with Heather at the moment,' I went on, revealing the crux of the problem. 'At least, she seems to be ignoring me a bit because she fancies Sam, despair, despair and she hangs round him all the time and chats him up. It makes me so jealous when people do that because I just have to stay where I am and wait for the bloke to come to me, which rarely happens . . . I think of Sam as a friend whom I love talking to but they seem to worship him . . . Even I who have talked to him several times, and that was when he mainly made the move, don't know what he's like deep down inside. It was just that his outward appearance was so friendly, kind, amusing and in short just how I like a boy to be. That's why I want to be with him or at least write to him so that I can find out about the real Sam. Now that I haven't seen him for so long I keep on conjuring up ideas about him, but I have to ask myself whether I really do like him or whether I'm just infatuated with him.' I was analysing everything even then.

When I was in my final year at university I grew very close to our lodger and there was a strong bond between us. After six months, jealousy reared its venomous head and had to be burned out of me through many an anguish-ridden trial. After the ashes had cooled we did become best buddies, but the scar tissue remained as a warning. At the beginning of the academic year Rosie came to stay and I prepared her to meet him. 'You'll be able to meet Jim, our lodger. He's been nicer recently. I expect he was just going through a manly phase before. We really are good friends but he is unpredictable and suddenly acts coldly and takes offence at something which he never minded me doing before . . . which is very hurtful. I kept fairly clear of him when he was acting strangely and recently he's actually invited me into his room several times. When you are here you won't notice any friction between Jim and me because he is always very nice with other people around. And as you are attractive and he's a real lad, he'll probably chat you up. He'll be on his best behaviour to make a good impression.'

My luck changed though and shortly after that I met my first boyfriend at a party in London. This guy was surprised I was not already married and poor Jim paled by comparison. More letters to Rosie showed that things were going well. 'I'm feeling happy at the moment because I saw my boyfriend, Ned, the other weekend and he is ten times nicer than Jim and good-looking besides, and we get on amazingly well. I stayed with friends in London and met Ned on Saturday. We spent a great day on a boat trip, going out for meals and drinks and to a party in the evening. My friends asked him to stay overnight in the flat so he left early on Sunday. Ned is ideal for me, because he has a deep understanding of disabled people. He was totally unembarrassed taking me to the loo and his attitude is amazing, quite happily taking me on the Underground, telling me I'm not at all demanding or presumptuous and giving me a whole list of reasons why he likes me. He even said I would be a nice person to take to France, whether he actually will though is a different matter . . .' Ned later revealed that he knew he wanted to go out with me as soon as he met me.

Sadly, it did not take long to discover that, however charming a man is, his words can be frustratingly empty. When Ned worked during the weekend he was due to come to Bristol for my birthday, my pen told the pain to Rosie: 'My pain was renewed today because I had a letter from Ned to say he was very sorry he wouldn't be able to come, etc. I wouldn't have minded if he had told me in the first place he might not be able to come and hadn't made it so definite. Now my pain is twice as deep because he made out he wasn't going to let me down. I don't know, these men. Honestly, there's not one of them that hasn't let me down. It's such a shame that Ned had to, because he's so good to me. I kept on thinking "Ned, not you, even you as well". Bit like "*Et tu, Brute*". Oh well. I'll get over it in time. I wouldn't mind so much if I knew when I was going to see him next . . . I am beginning to become a cynic as far as men are concerned, but then something happens to restore my faith in them and then I get hurt again . . .'

It has to be said that I was often on the receiving end of men's unwelcome passion, but I had little sympathy for their unrequited love. I found the whole situation so awkward. I preferred to deny their feelings. I asked one poor man to take me out to lunch but when he wanted to kiss me I was a granite stone of denial. I enjoyed his flattering attention and being told I was beautiful, up to a point, but it wasn't fair on me or him to pretend otherwise. I received hilariously passionate letters from one smitten admirer (he swore it was love at first sight) for a while, which was rather wonderful, but in the end I had to put a stop to it. I wrote to a friend once after having been a little harassed by someone who fancied me, 'The guy who came to stay that weekend has just phoned . . . I haven't replied to his letter or birthday card – oh dear.' Oh dear, indeed, I should have known better how he felt.

Thus, throughout my late teens and early twenties, I had met men and developed relationships, but not without lengthy periods of being haunted by the crushing torment of loneliness and longing. Out of my first period of emotional isolation emerged a creative flow. I was surprised at how many poems I found lurking in my old diary. They express excruciating pain and most have no worth other than as a cathartic exercise.

The man who gave rise to a whole book of love poems was Dorian. I met him at an actors' party at the Arts Centre Group, on January 13th, 1984. He had rung me the day before because he was organising food contributions for the party. I thought it opportune to let him know I was in a wheelchair so he could meet me and give me a hand up the steps. He stood me up! When he came to apologise for forgetting, we clicked immediately and he wasn't fazed when I told him I was an actress. He took it for granted that my wheelchair made no difference to my professional ability. He invited himself round to show me his India photos, and took my telephone number. I went to bed feeling, 'This is it, I've met him!' I pleaded with God not to let my love be unrequited. I could already imagine my life with Dorian but it was nearly a year before we began to see each other regularly. Both he and I were acting out of London throughout the year. We were seldom able to meet and I actually went off him for a while, telling Jim, 'I can't cope with his traditional views of the woman's role, marriage, etc, and his admiration for Mrs Thatcher. Now that I am getting to know him, he's got some really annoying streaks. I guess I'll never find someone who understands me or takes the trouble to, like you, but then I don't want you for my sexual partner, so that's not much use.'

It was a year after Dorian and I first met, to the very day, January 13th, 1985, when we started going out. Dorian had stayed with me in Bristol for New Year and that had brought us very close. He had sent a 'thank you' note to my parents saying, 'Ellen is a marvellous friend for me to have, we share an extraordinary number of interests.'

Everything came to a head one night when he was round and I had to go out to a party. We had kissed goodbye before I left my flat and Dorian felt the strength of my feelings and said he did not feel the same for me. On my return I found a hand-delivered note from Dorian, apologising for any insensitivity and stating, 'I do love you as a friend and as a friend in Jesus. Please may we continue?' I cried and prayed in anguish to God and went through a dark night of the soul at the prospect of giving up my dream. The next day we met again and we seemed to grow closer not further apart. I had written to Dorian a few months previously, saying that I thought he was holding something back and now he admitted that he was! He found it hard to cope with my being so free, open and physical. The following day was the 13th, the big day. I went round to his place and we spent the afternoon looking at photographs. In the evening I had a poetry reading to do and he came with me. After the gig he took me home in his car. I was expecting to be delivered home with a sedate platonic kiss, but Dorian took it from the platonic to the romantic!

One of the advantages of being unable to walk is that men often have to carry me in their arms. The disadvantage is that this has become mundane and so it has lost its romantic edge, but in certain situations the necessity thrust upon us can add that extra touch of the romantic that able-bodied couples would not have. It would not be common practice for able-bodied couples to carry their partner from their car to their door! I looked up into his face, we kissed and I said, 'Who needs words?' He replied, 'Yes, exactly!' We became a couple. Our relationship developed and deepened and my flatmate, Helena, said that she felt she was watching something wonderful unfold.

Late in 1985 we spent a month together at L'Abri in Switzerland. L'Abri is the French word for 'Shelter', which exactly describes the community. It is a haven in the Alps where you study part-time any God-related topic from music to mysticism and work part-time in the fields or chalets. It was a great opportunity for us to work on certain aspects of our relationship and we spent many happy hours together. The epitome of ecstasy for me was being alone with Dorian, surrounded by the beauty of the mountains and listening to music from the Taizé community on his Walkman. But the course of true love never ran smooth. Even then we had already experienced deep pain and some bitter conflicts.

Right from the very beginning people created difficulties and problems for us because of their prejudices. Society, as a whole, finds it difficult to accept that able-bodied and disabled people can make good sexual partners. The church, in particular, instead of being in the forefront of enlightened opinion, lags behind. Sadly, most of the attacks came from Christians and this appeared to give their opposition more significance in Dorian's eyes. No sooner had Dorian mentioned that he was going out with me than he was told it was out of sympathy. My flatmate Helena was furious. 'SYMPATHY! Someone said that after meeting you once? That's just sick. So he's got a hot line to God, has he? For a Christian to say something like that, I'd seriously question where he is coming from!' I wrote a letter to Dorian in the early hours of the morning after that conversation. 'You can tell him that I was born able-bodied, brought up in a totally able-bodied environment, never met anyone "disabled", always had able-bodied boyfriends, and he's going round with his mind in a wheelchair! He needs to be reminded that he is only a T.A.B. (temporarily ablebodied) himself . . . Who is he to judge whether "it's right" when God has brought us together? I wondered why that phrase. "Those whom God hath joined together let no man put asunder" was going through my mind all day long.' My mother warned me too that people might criticise out of jealousy. Others who might be fond of Dorian would find it harder to accept me as his girlfriend and my disability gave people a convenient lever with which to try to separate us.

Even the vicar was no ally. He suggested that 'we leave God out of this'. Oh yes, and bring Him back in when it's convenient, no doubt! I could not cope with the vicar's contradiction: on the one hand I was asexual and not supposed to be sexually fulfilled and on the other I was seen as a terrible temptress who should not be touched. Either way I was in the 'wrong'. Dorian and I were forced to consider our relationship more deeply than many other couples are ever expected to. We had to face issues that would have been taken for granted by two ablebodied people. I felt degraded by the level of discussion and outside comment on our lives and believed it was insulting God to deny my sexuality. My disability is not separate from me, it is me. I am who I am, I am my body created in God's image and God made all people sexual beings. I challenged the assumption that my sexual ability was different. The lack of imagination of the general public often amazes me when they ask me whether or not I can have sex. If they have to ask that question their sex lives must be very boring.

Right at the very beginning people were taking it upon themselves to be Dorian's marriage guidance counsellor, or rather his anti-marriage counsellor. However, as Helena rightly pointed out, we were hardly contemplating marriage at that stage. 'Marriage!' she exclaimed. 'You've only been going out for a few days, for goodness sake. How can you know someone is right to marry if you don't go out with them? I get so angry with these people who pressurise Christian relationships. They take it so seriously, e.g. "Let's have a prayer meeting to see if we should have a prayer meeting to see if you can hold hands". God must look down in despair and think, "It's supposed to be fun, okay? Enjoy it."'

One of the first Christian responses to Dorian, when he mentioned that he was going out with me, was, 'Is she going to be healed?' When my parents used to go to the Christian Dental Fellowship Conferences my mother dreaded every time that someone would suggest they take me for healing. They prepared themselves and decided that if I wanted to ask for healing for myself when I was an adult, then that was fine. It was typical of their altruism in not trying to impose something on me for their own sakes. Many Christians believe that disability is a wrong state and that it should not be tolerated or accepted. God's people are supposed to be healthy, well off and protected, and if they are not they must have done something wrong. In its simplest form they see illness and affliction as perhaps having been brought on by the sin of the individual. If healing is not forthcoming, that too is an indication of the disabled person's lack of faith. The whole attitude is a very convenient way to avoid looking at one's own prejudices.

On a train journey home after seeing Dorian in a show I met a man who exemplified this philosophy perfectly. The man came up to me and started chatting to me. He told me that he was a preacher and I told him I was a Christian. He had just come from a Pentecostal conference and I immediately thought, 'Oh, here we go, he's going to tell me to get healed.' My reflex reaction was right. The problem was that he was extremely arrogant and came out with the most outrageous, and to me almost blasphemous, comments. I could have coped with what he was saying if I had felt human warmth from him and if he had spoken out of love. I was almost willing him to be loving, but there was no sign of it. Hammer, hammer, hammer, it was all theory and no awareness of me as a person. It was as if he had become so caught up in his conference that as soon as he saw me he thought, 'Ah, quick, catch the crip – opportunity to heal and get in as many Bible quotes as I can at the same time – to show I studied it for a year'. I am sure he knew the Bible better than me as a text, but at least I do try and listen to what God is telling me through it. He wasn't interested in hearing my viewpoint on suffering, or what I had learnt through experience, or what I felt was God's will for me. He told me that he 'knew' what God's will for me was.

As he carried on I desperately prayed for the right words to show that I had some Christian understanding as I tried to explain my point of view. Fortunately I had just been reading about affliction that day, so much of that was fresh in my memory and it was really helpful. He told me that I could do more for God if I were able-bodied. I am convinced that if that were the case then I would not have been born with muscular dystrophy. He implied that he was a better person than me because he was 'whole' and I was not, which I dispute. I told him I didn't feel any less human, nor would I necessarily be happier if I could walk. He asked me did I think that God had missing arms and missing legs. I told him I didn't think God had arms or legs at all. He finished up laying hands on me and praying for wholeness of my body, mind and soul and he commanded the devil to leave me and so forth. I accepted his prayer in all humil-

148

ity. A week later I read in Timothy that one should be humble and courteous to those with wrong ideas, for then they are more likely to believe what is true. Even though I did not know that passage at the time it was exactly what had been going through my mind when I spoke with this man and why I was desperately trying to be polite all the time.

When I tried to explain to him what I believed about suffering, I remembered an example from Roger Hurding's book *As Trees Walking*. He described God as a master weaver who is making a beautiful tapestry with the lives of his people throughout history. Individual believers and the Church generally may not appreciate that there is a loving design involved while they are undergoing affliction. It is as if, for most of the time, we can only see the obverse of the artwork where the skeins of silk seem to make little sense in terms of colour and pattern. In my relationship with Dorian I would very soon need that picture. Just as I also found very helpful Susan Schaeffer Macaulay's description of herself as a child painting a picture. She had almost finished her picture when she dropped a large blob of red paint down the middle of the canvas. She was just about to scrap the whole project when her mother came in and told her not to destroy it, but instead to find a way of using the red paint in the picture. She said God always got a paint-spattered picture to work with.

While much damage was done to Dorian and me by people's thoughtless comments, the trauma proved our love and I wrote to Dorian, 'As I experience the ocean depths and the sky's breadths and the mountain heights of my love, and I reflect that God's love for us is ten million times greater, I think WOW! Depths of love bring deep fulfilment and deep happiness. And there's no short cut, it can certainly never be reached by sex alone.' On the other hand, the outside comment on our relationship was, at times, unbearable. Even if we spent a weekend together, just with my family, people implied it was wrong. They forced the issue for us when to have the

149

question of marriage hanging over us at this stage was unnecessary.

Dorian amazed me sometimes, for he was so sensitive to certain practical aspects of my disability. After our first venture into a public loo, I told him, 'I feel I furthered your education today by our trip to the Ladies! I have experienced it a lot with other blokes and I really feel for them having to go into forbidden territory for my sake. Many people don't think about pulling the flush or that I might want to wash my hands afterwards, things they do for themselves without thinking.' But other aspects Dorian found difficult, particularly my habit of being straightforward with people about my disability. 'What I lack in muscle I make up for in mouth,' I wrote in my diary after Dorian had been shocked at the way I snapped at a British Rail porter who quizzed me on whether I would be all right travelling on my own. How else can I prove my capability in a brief moment except by telling people? Similarly when I was bought an ice cream by a stranger in Covent Garden, Dorian had said 'bless you' and I had said to Dorian, 'You have it, I don't want it.' I wrote to him afterwards, 'You know I was screaming inside when that man bought me an ice cream. So please, please don't say "Bless you" to such acts of charity, however well meaning they are. You only add insult to injury and it doesn't help people to have the right attitude.'

In the same way as I had been forced to surrender my teenage ideals and romantic dreams, Dorian was having to learn to give up his ideal woman. He wrote to me: 'It's pride that I'm finding it so hard to come to terms with going out with someone disabled. That hazy vague phrase "someone disabled" is what does the damage because the lovely you is clouded by a general image of a wheelchair and that's because I'm worried about me and not about you.' Though by the end of the letter he had written 'I know you are there in my heart'.

Yet again it was Helena who was so wonderfully helpful and supportive at this time. She pointed out to me, from an objective point of view, the problems an able-bodied person might have in relating to me. I, myself, can't undo all my knowledge of disability and become ignorant. She told me how, at the start of the time when she came to live with me, she used to panic and get feelings of claustrophobia. It was simply because I was an unknown quantity and she did not know what she had to do for me. She hadn't realised how much I could do for myself and said that it was only through living with me that she forgot totally that I was disabled. It's only now if she sees the fear on other people's faces that she is reminded, 'Oh yes, Ellen can't walk.'

It was because being in a wheelchair had such a stigma attached to it that I fought for so long not to have to use one. I refused to use a wheelchair because that image wasn't me and I didn't want to be a part of it. After all, if you put an able-bodied person in a wheelchair they immediately look disabled. It's only in recent years that I have succumbed, for practical reasons, to using a wheelchair and I look upon it as a form of transport. Ironically, visual impact is not always what makes people afraid. Often the object of fear produces greater terror in the imagination than is warranted.

Dorian had warned me that his parents would not be at all happy about our relationship, but I knew that there would come a time when he would have to tell them and it was my turn to fear. I wrote, 'Dorian, I'm afraid of not being accepted by your parents. I may have to accept I'll never be accepted.' I hit the nail on the head. I little knew the extent of the antagonism ahead.

I felt strongly that he should not tell his parents without letting them meet me first. I wrote to him and said so. 'In fact, I would really like to be there when you tell them. Of course you must decide whatever is best, they are your parents and it is easier for you . . . The reason I think they should meet me first is because they can only see the chair and not me . . . Also, hopefully, if we're there together they might see the bond between us. I'm sure they would. People who are elderly or who haven't come into direct contact with disability have the worst preconceptions, so it will be difficult with your parents I think, but walls can be broken down.'

A few days after my intuition of non-acceptance, Dorian rang. He had told his parents and the results had not been good. After a long and agonised conversation I put the phone down, crumbled into tears and fell into Helena's arms crying, 'I can't bear it, I knew, I knew, it would be like this. Everybody else said it would be all right, but I knew.' We prayed together. All I remember is Helena saying, 'May the wheelchair in their mind be dimmed and may they only see the vibrant and beautiful person she is.'

I wrote to Dorian the next morning. 'I don't know what to say or how to comfort you . . . More than anything I wish I could be with you. The aching pain that I feel is intensified by our separation.' I flung a few pages into the post along with a poem.

As a cloud pours soothing rain
to bring relief
and cool hot pain
death brings resurrection
so through pangs of birth
we can start to live again
So I can survive
in the tunnel's darkness
as long as I can glimpse a glimmer of light
companion to the fight

I felt sick and tired and could not bear seeing our peace and happiness destroyed all the time. I feared Dorian would resent me because of his parents' violent reaction. At the same time I was angry because events were out of my control. 'How can you expect them to see anything more than a wheelchair when the flesh and blood woman is nothing to them!' I exclaimed. In the same way, his parents were not flesh and blood people to me, so my real disability was how to love them when I felt at the time

152

that I positively loathed them! Luckily, my intuition about how they would react prepared me and helped me enormously.

Helena pointed out that my disability was not entirely to blame, but that it highlighted certain things in all our relationships. It acted as a scapegoat for problems that people do not want to face in themselves. It is not easy to sweep a wheelchair under the carpet as one would a drink problem or a violent temper. Also, some parents seem determined to find fault in the most eligible of partners. I know someone whose mother's comment on his girlfriend was, 'She's very nice but she has got the most irritating cough,' as if she had to pick on something. Towards the end of our relationship Dorian commented that he would never have learned so much if it wasn't for my disability. Nor could he escape the fact that my disability made me the person he liked. Amidst all my anger I still felt for Dorian and his pain. I wrote, 'I realise that for myself it would not deeply matter if they never accepted me, as I could take it, but I want them to for you,' and I told Dorian that if his parents could come to know Christ through all this, then our suffering was worth it. That all sounds rather noble in retrospect, but I meant it. I longed for that day. I never got to meet them though. The first and last communication I received from Dorian's mother was a touching poem she wrote about me before she realised that we were going out. I treasure it and keep it by my bed.

One redeeming factor for both of us amidst the family rows was the staunch support of Dorian's brother who thought I was great news for Dorian. Though he found it tough to speak out to his parents he was not reluctant to do so. He also told Dorian that if we did decide to get married it would be a good move. Thank God for a voice of humanity above the clamour of negativity. What a pity it could not have come from within the Church.

After L'Abri, in the autumn of 1985, we became much closer and more deeply in love. We had even got to the stage of generally talking about marriage and children.

Apart from my name being a forbidden subject in Dorian's family home, we were at the peak of our happiness and my poems were prolific.

I have never wanted children. I think they are too demanding. It is not that I don't like children, I simply don't want to be a mother. I love my nieces and nephews as if they were my own children and I think they are wonderful because, unlike adults, they are not at all precious about disability. I told my nephew Peter, when he was three, not to take my tablets because they would make him ill. A bit later on he asked what I took the tablets for. 'To make me better,' I said. He replied instantly, 'Did you take some tablets to make you ill, so now you have these tablets to make you better, Aunty Aylin?' But to have my own children would be a different matter. Dorian, however, said he really wanted a family so I had to consider the matter and I came to the conclusion that I did love this man enough to go through pregnancy for him. Even so, I went to the doctor to ask for her advice, half in the hope that she would tell me it wasn't medically a good idea. On the contrary, she told me, no reason why not, although I would probably have to have a Caesarean.

Thus, while Dorian and I began to talk about the implications of a permanent relationship, his parents grew more and more anxious and antagonistic. He was torn between their reaction and his love for me, so perhaps some of his subsequent mental illness was an attempt to find a way out of what seemed to be an impossible situation.

The exact nature of his illness is a highly sensitive issue and I have to respect his privacy, especially since he is not yet free of its effects. As far as he understands it, it is, to use his words, 'a form of spiritual attack resulting in mental distress'. It first manifested itself in erratic behaviour. He had always been a faithful Christian and sought God's will in everything, but now he began to tell me we were not 'meant' to go out on specific nights. God, he said, had told him so directly. While the warning signs were there, the whole process was interrupted by his mother's sudden death.

The news came to him as he was about to perform in the first night of his own show. I had sent him a dozen red roses as an indication of my love and support. He rang to say that his mother was dying and then rang a few hours later to say that she had died and that he would put the roses I had sent him on her grave.

Tapestry

I knew
in different towns and yet
I knew
the whole day through
there was something wrong
very wrong with you
my emotions told me

But death.
I could not have guessed
death
so grim and fast
most unwelcome uninvited guest
who tears and grasps
at every heart

I knew
the flowers were right to send you
I knew
but little thought they were for her
a reconciliation gift for a mother
a hello and goodbye
agape on a grave

I'm looking at a tapestry
I see many loose strands and threads
and multi-coloured humpy knots
a tangled mess quite ugly

that's my view
from behind
my eyes are not yet privileged to scan
the whole masterpiece
as yet unknown to man

He told me then that he loved me and I ran to Helena to tell her. It was the first time I had heard those three words for quite a while.

Dorian's mother had died of cancer. She had experienced some back pain but a diagnosis had come too late to do anything and its progress was shockingly rapid. For a while this terrible event seemed to bring Dorian back to his former self. However, the voices that had haunted him before and told him what to do soon returned. By now the symptoms were so marked and frightening that his father and brother wanted him to seek professional help.

In the end he went to see a psychiatrist in London. He rang me the night before he was due to go and I offered to go with him to the appointment. He agreed and came round that day. We spent some time together beforehand as if nothing was wrong, except that he could not talk about 'us'. Then we caught a cab and we sat holding hands. He was very stiff and tense and I was afraid to ask him to put his arm around me in case it worried him, although every time we went round a corner I thought I was going to fall off the seat. I left him at the hospital and went back in the cab. The psychiatrist made a diagnosis and prescribed medication which gave him hope but he found the side effects unbearable.

When some kind of diagnosis and explanation of his behaviour was finally offered, I felt at once both shocked and relieved. It was comforting to know that his behaviour had some kind of explanation and was not the result of a change of feeling towards me. I began to write a journal to try and help me come to terms with what was happening and in it I wrote, 'Day 4: I move round my flat in a daze, a haze of unreality, I feel as if I am inside a bubble and one day I will burst through to the outside to reality. I feel flat but my emotions are up and down like a yo-yo. Day 5: A friend of my mother's comes for lunch and distracts my mind for a while. I'm forced to be sociable, I offer drinks, pretending to be the perfect hostess without a care in the world. Day 7 and 9: I leave with my mother to go to Bristol for a long weekend and escape. As the train moves out of Paddington it's warm and sunny and I am so glad to be "leaving my situation behind" that tears of relief trickle down my cheeks and I think "I don't ever want to come back". The problem is when I arrive in Bristol, I haven't really left my situation behind. In church on Sunday a hymn turns on my tear tap, "When through the deep waters He calls me to go, the rivers of grief will not me overflow." If they get any deeper I will drown.'

However, it was a huge relief to feel the responsibility lifted from my shoulders in the realisation that no persuasion on my part could change him. I just had to wait. Sadly, in the summer of 1986, he went into hospital for a while and only wanted his family to visit him. However, we were still very close and wrote long letters to each other. I wrote several poems.

Being There

all those who have been
to that barren land
where there are no trees
to shade from the blistering heat
and no shelters from the biting wind
where darkness covers the land at day
with no respite
when you can't find a switch
to turn on any light

know that I have been there too
and there my face launched a thousand tears
on which I sailed to clearer sight

brought back renewed
though not without a fight

and always you think you're alone
but you never are
there's always someone near
hidden in the dark
though not hiding
impossible for the eye to see
though not invisible deliberately

all those who are there
know that I am being there
with you

In a letter Dorian wrote, 'I am not able to make decisions at present, because I have not got the strength to follow them.' Only I realised the significance of that statement at the time.

Once out of hospital, Dorian decided to go on holiday for six weeks to take a break and recover. But he did not come back. He went missing. His brother alerted the authorities and Interpol in France finally found him. As a result he hardly had a holiday, more of a nightmare. His brother flew out to bring him back to England and Dorian went back to hospital, for a long stay this time.

Not to be outdone, I also ended up in hospital. Mine was a decidedly shorter stay, though. I was returning to London from my parents' home in Bristol, and reached the station on time but British Rail did not take me on to the platform until too late. In my desperate haste, I sped up a ramp and my wheelchair did a backwards half somersault and I split my head open and had to have nine stitches. Needless to say, I did not catch the train, although I tried to, and it was only the blood that shocked me into realising the extent of the damage. I thought I had got off scot free.

I visited Dorian at last though, bandaged head and all. I tried to see him as often as I could, a few times a week.

After some weeks I was surprised to find that patients and staff were convinced that we were engaged. People came up to me and congratulated me on the 'good news' although it was the first I had heard of it. I didn't want him to run before he could walk. In fact Dorian had merely intimated that he wanted to marry me which is hardly a formal engagement. It was hard to leave at the end of a visit – I wanted to take him with me. Those times together were a wonderful opportunity to just 'be'. It reminded me of a letter I had written to him earlier in our relationship: 'The more I am with you the more it becomes important just to BE with you. Of secondary importance is talking, sharing. Thirdly "doing" things together, and of those things the more "passive" are the more special e.g., looking at the countryside or watching ducks on a pond!'

Later on, after Dorian came out of hospital, he said he wanted to marry me and on another occasion actually asked me. He came to stay with me at my parents' home for a week at New Year and for the week before that. When I had been without him I had not really missed him or longed for him and I began to have nagging doubts that I could commit myself to him for life. Doubts were emerging in Dorian, too. By the end of the week together we concluded that it was indeed over, but it was hard to admit. Dorian was so loving to me and poured out a stream of compliments. 'You're beautiful, attractive, intelligent and have a lovely personality . . .' We carried on seeing each other regularly for about a year and are still friends. It may not be easy to acknowledge that you can't live with someone but it is far more painful to be forced to live without them – thus the agony of divorce.

Ex

Funny to think you're
just another 'ex' to add to the list
when you're anything but
'just another ex to add to the list'

Textured visions of our past holding-hand happiness
torment me with their beautiful simplicity
but like a bitter sweet draught
I could not choose to leave the cup standing
or let my lips stay dry

Our lives were intertwined
on the verge of the sacred vows
unpicking the twine
takes more than time
don't pull so fast
that I spin in dizzy turns
that you suffer rope burns
We still have skin grafts
yours to mine
mine to yours
some will stay
and it should remain that way
and it shall remain that way

For both of us it was the happiest few years of our lives
and nobody can take that away from us. I don't know if I
will ever be so happy again. I believe it is possible but I
simply find it hard to imagine because what we had was
so special and in some ways far beyond the level that
many couples reach in their marriages. I called my book
of love poems for Dorian *Eternal Love* which is a bold title,
but I was convinced it would be the one true everlasting
love of my life and I invested everything in it. We are still
fond of each other and always will be, but even that
seems a pretty bold statement. Dorian gave me my most
precious and most painful memories. I choose to retain
the precious. They are the only important ones, after all.

12

'Once upon a time in your wildest dreams?'
Anon

Shortly after leaving Graeae in the autumn of 1984 an artistic director who had seen me perform offered me a job with the Half Moon Young People's Theatre. I told a friend I was 'over the half moon', because it was a company of able-bodied actors and I felt I had escaped the ghetto. It was a two-month project which sowed the seeds of an exciting new integrated company which sprouted in 1985/86.

Nic, ex-director of Graeae, who was employed to direct the show, suggested that we invite two other disabled actors, as well as me, to give a better balance to the company and give a chance to more actors with disabilities. Up until then I was really pleased at the thought of not working with disabled actors because I saw it as a real breakthrough for me. However, I saw his point. We devised the show from scratch with two weeks of workshops and four weeks for scripting and rehearsals, plus two weeks of performance. It was exciting and challenging to be working alongside able-bodied actors and, looking back, it was a scene from my wildest childhood dreams. The show, *Spinning a Yarn*, was wonderful, something meaty to get my teeth into and very different form from any theatre piece I had done previously. We didn't perform it for the general public, but mainly in community centres. As it was Christmas time, we tended to get booked as their Christmas show which wasn't entirely appropriate. We got a few comments like, 'It was a bit too cultural for me,' but that was from someone who missed the first half hour because the nurse came to 'do his foot'. One venue was decidedly Dickensian. It looked like a workhouse: some of the audience were dragged out halfway through and they were miserly enough to charge us for a cup of tea.

A handful of us from that two-month project thought the show really deserved a decent run in proper theatre venues, so we founded the 'Double Exposure' theatre company in order to apply for funding for the venture. The title of the company was born from a play on words and concepts. Apart from the obvious idea of media exposure, there was the idea of double exposure on a film. This is usually unintentional, but it can be brilliant. Actors with disabilities can be subjected to over-exposure to publicity or lack of exposure to the public; the title encapsulated the idea of the double exposure of both talent and disability.

We were the first professional integrated theatre company in Britain to get off the ground properly. We had a policy of integrating other minorities too. *Spinning a Yarn* was re-written and re-cast and we toured London theatres from February to March 1986.

Just when I had no idea what was on the horizon apart from sitting at home and writing poetry, and I was at a low ebb in many ways, I received one of those magic out-of-the-blue phone calls. How would I like to be a television presenter? said a voice on the other end.

In 1980 I had written to Rosie about a similar offer I had had from a producer in Radio Bristol: 'He asked me if I had ever thought of being a presenter and he wants me to present his programme. He's thinking of sending me out to interview people. Help! That's the one thing I can't imagine myself doing! He said he'd been looking for someone like me for a long time. I expect he's pretty desperate by now and willing to take anybody.' Six years later the offer from the producer of *Same Difference* made me react differently, which goes to show how much one can change. Until I saw my older letter recently I had totally forgotten that I had previously been considered for presenting a programme. I had never really liked seeing myself on television either and had always been very critical of how I came across during the occasional television slot. When I saw myself on *Spotlight South West* on tour I wrote, 'It was quite horrendous. I never want to be on T.V. again, but I probably will be.' How prophetic! However it is not every day of the week one is offered a Channel 4 presentation job, even if it was taking me out of the integrated atmosphere of Double Exposure and back into the ghetto of minority broadcasting. *Same Difference* is a magazine programme on topical issues related to disability.

I didn't just 'walk' into it. The producer told me first of all that I had to provide a video to assess my suitability for television. By a stroke of luck I had presented a video on sign language for Nic. Someone had said at the time, 'Ellen would make a good T.V. presenter.' When my video performance was approved, the producer proceeded to inform me that he already had somebody else in mind for the job and that he would probably use him. That really boosted my confidence! But he still wanted me to audition so it was now up to me to make myself indispensable to him. I had to do a mock interview and practise reading from an autocue.

After the audition, the commissioning editor from Channel 4 came in and started asking me questions. He was curious about my motives for wanting to become a television presenter when my first profession was acting. I knew personally that it would be a good career move because long theatre tours are very wearing and I wanted to work in London in order to have the appropriate physical back-up and home comforts. Touring is a brilliant experience when you are young, free and single and full of energy. I wasn't exactly long in the tooth, but I had reached the point where three weeks' rehearsal – sometimes working six days a week and learning lines every evening – was draining my reserves. I had little left for the rigours of touring.

Television is hardly easy-going, as I was soon to discover. After passing the audition, the next stage was recording the pilot programme. Only then would the producer be granted air-time and a full budget.

I had been told I would be sent the script before we went into the studio to record, so as to have a chance to familiarise myself with its contents. When it did not arrive I was worried I would look stupid, so I turned up at the studio in a panic, apologising and saying I had not received the script. 'Oh that's all right,' said the producer. 'I didn't send one to you.' I was relieved because I knew I hadn't missed something vital, but I felt that it gave my co-presenter an advantage over me as he knew the script well, having written it.

I had a headache that morning and I didn't manage to get a breather at lunch time because they brought food in for us. By the time I had munched through my roll we were due to start work again. We were in the same studio all day with no windows, no fresh air and no natural light. The hot studio lights made the atmosphere very oppressive and it aggravated my headache so that in between sessions I just laid my head back on the chair and closed my eyes. At the end of the afternoon I was horrified at what people would think of apparently falling asleep on such a vital day. Here was the 'conscientious' little girl of my childhood seeping through. I felt it must have made a rather poor impression because the producer could see me from the control box, even though I could not see him. Consequently, I had not been very aware of him until he came into the studio. However, when he kindly helped me into the taxi I was surprised to hear him say I was really, really good, he would definitely be in touch. I had not blotted my copybook, after all. I left feeling confident. The producer was obviously pleased with my performance in the pilot and I had a new job on the horizon. Moreover, I hadn't even made the effort of lifting the phone or filling in an application form.

When I saw the pilot and took a cold, hard look at my performance I saw a lot of faults. But we got the series so I can't have let the side down too badly, and the schedule was certainly an improvement on touring. Time-wise it was not taxing at all. We were only in the studio once a week, every Saturday, and the programme was transmitted on the following Monday. I was perfectly content working on a Saturday because it meant that the London traffic into Channel 4's West End studios was quite bearable. It was not a long day either. I usually finished at lunch time, but very occasionally I had an interview or extra snippet of work in the afternoon. Apart from that, I only regularly worked two evenings a week.

During the first series I sometimes went into the television company's London office to do odd bits of work, including reading all the viewers' letters which was like a delve into a fascinating treasure trove. Being used to performing, it meant a lot to me to see the audience feedback. I was not used to receiving fan mail and requests for photographs of me too.

We decided on the title *Same Difference* after much discussion. We had originally been thinking about titles like *Not the Six o'clock News* because we were at a peak six o'clock slot, which was great because we were not shoved in a ghetto viewing time. However trying to say a title that began *Not the . . .* was not easy, and 'Tonight on *Not the Six o'clock News . . .*' was too much of a mouthful. Besides, the repeat was at nine-thirty on a Saturday morning, so the title would have looked more than a little daft then. I came up with the title *Same Difference* when I was chewing over something pithy which would both embody disability in an allusive way and not alienate non-disabled viewers.

On one of my rare chances to go on location, I went abroad to Benidorm. The producer had wangled a week's Horizon holiday for me and a helper so I could report on access and facilities for disabled people willing to chance a stay in Benidorm. The shoot was very enjoyable but only took three days so the rest of the week was ours to spend by ourselves in the resort. Well, it was a very nice thought and a great idea – but Benidorm?

For a start the weather was not that hot. I had planned to stretch out on the beach and do some serious sunbathing, but it was cold and grey and actually rained one day. I hadn't brought enough books with me to cover for sitting in the hotel and reading. The hotel itself was one of those large tacky monstrosities, all concrete and anodised aluminium like something from one of your wildest nightmares, or mine anyway. Its position was such that you might just as well have stretched out to sunbathe in the middle of the street. It was hardly idyllic lying by the pool, breathing in exhaust fumes from the cars and lorries rumbling past. It's not a question of being grateful or ungrateful. It is a job and you can't complain if you are paid to be there, but I don't want the viewers to get any false ideas of 'stars' in 'glamorous' spots having a doss. It was a mainly English resort so there was plenty of fish and chips, lager louts and English pubs. It was like a little Britain in Benidorm and inspired a song.

Benidorm

They've built a little Britain in Benidorm
they've built a little Britain except it's rich English fellas
who can't stand paellas warm
they've built a little Britain in Benidorm.

Hamburgers and piano bars
fish and chips and greasy spoons
British pubs and British grub
British discos with British tunes.

M and S and C and A
with rows and rows of British clothes
fag machines and fruit machines
and British kids having British goes.

When the reporting came to an end and the crew were shortly to leave, I was begging them, 'Please let me come with you'. I was joking because it wasn't an option, but I have honestly never been so glad to come home from a holiday in all my life.

The most interesting aspect of Benidorm for me personally was being recognised as a media personality. Amazingly, British tourists recognised me in the streets or the hotel and thought we were filming a follow-up to *Raspberry Ripple* because it had been on air two weeks previously. In contrast, one of the 'carpet-slippers, curlers and crimplene' crowd who lived in Benidorm said to my helper, Helen, that I was brave and didn't she feel sorry for me? Helen replied, 'No I don't. She's got a very good job. She's better paid than me, she's got her own place and she's happier than most people I know.'

I discovered that my battery-powered chair had been given preferential treatment by the airline because we were filming for Channel 4. A woman at our hotel who travelled with the same airline had only been permitted her manual wheelchair and her granddaughter to push her. If I had been travelling merely as Ellen Wilkie, disabled person, rather than as Elly Wilkie, television presenter, I would have received the same treatment and such needless discrimination makes my blood boil. To discriminate against someone due to their disability is bad enough, but to discriminate because they do not have the professional clout of a film crew in tow is sick.

After similar experiences in Turkey, I mused on the pros and cons of being recognised. When I was recognised from my television appearances, people could relate to me much more as an equal than they often did when my wheelchair loomed larger in their eyes than my person. For instance, my ability to talk is already recognised and they know that I can hold down not only a decent job but a television career as well. This has such kudos attached to it that I am treated as an equal. So any statements are of the 'I've seen you on T.V.' variety and any questions are of the 'When is your next T.V. appearance?' type. Sometimes these are not so easy to answer if there is no T.V. slot looming on the horizon. It took me a while to realise that recognition breaks down barriers so swiftly. How vital then is representative employment of people with disabilities in television. *Same Difference* is of particular interest to people with disabilities, but it is aimed at a wider audience, too. Judging from the letters alone, it certainly appeals to able-bodied people. The response from them was very gratifying. One person wrote in immediately after watching only the first programme, saying his attitude towards people in wheelchairs had changed completely. He would never look upon them in the same way again. Many people wrote in and asked why we were not presenting mainstream programmes. Why did we have to be restricted to serving the disabled community? If disabled people were integrated into mainstream television, I wonder if the need for separate slots would disappear. It certainly begs the question. The letters from our viewers were a fascinating eye-opener. Producers often say that they can't use a disabled person in a programme with no specific axe to grind because the audience are not ready to accept a disabled person presenting the *Six O'clock News* or *Blue Peter*. But on the contrary, our letters revealed that the audience is well ahead of the producers and would very happily accept a disabled person presenting or working on any number of programmes. Actually our commissioning editor backed up that response when he commented after the first series that other Channel 4 programmes should snap us up. Personally, I'd like a stab at *That's Life* or *Jackanory* or both, even though they are not on Channel 4.

In the end I chose not to do a third series. I had received another offer from elsewhere but made my decision before signing a contract with a different producer. I did not expect a television job to be perfect, free of tension or exhaustive of my talent but, weighing up the pros and cons, I decided where to draw the line. That's not to say it was easy. Television presenter's jobs are hard to come by, and male producers are more likely to go for leggy airheads than wheely bright sparks. It was one of the major decisions of my life and a lonely one, too. I loved being a television presenter and I honestly don't think I could have had the strength to do what I knew was right without God's help. I was reading about David and Goliath at the time and how David had stood firm against all 'reasonable' discussion.

Fortunately I had found an agent by then, which helped, and a few people who knew the situation supported me. Later, when my 'other offer' materialised and I was also invited back to *Same Difference*, my stand had proved right.

As for my agent, it was a feather in her cap that she saw no difficulty in putting me up for any job other than the type that required acrobatics or juggling. That's what I call integration!

The moment she agreed to take me on I felt a load lifted from my shoulders. No longer would I have to spend hours making endless phone calls chasing up elusive producers and being fobbed off with 'he's in a meeting, editing, out' and so forth. Of course, as the old adage goes, what you gain on the swings you lose on the roundabouts. Having an agent working for you is a relationship of trust. Unless you get called for auditions and interviews there is no way of knowing that your agent is actually pursuing jobs on your behalf. All in all, though, the advantages outweigh the disadvantages. Most advantageous is the avoidance of media manipulation. A producer may commission you to write a piece to present to camera, say, and then ask you to make unreasonable changes. Your agent can step in and say, 'Stop messing my client about.' It's bad enough if you're well experienced in the media. What about the poor innocent victims who are new to it all?

My television experiences did not end with *Same Difference*. I have had the chance to do some non-disability orientated work for Television South (T.V.S.) as well as for the B.B.C. As a result of an article written about me in the *Independent* the producer of the B.B.C. programme

Five to Eleven booked me for a slot. It is a five-minute programme where actors read poems. It has no reference to disability at all and so it was great for me to break the mould and feel treated as an equal. The offer came out of the blue and I was in my element reading poetry. I had the opportunity to read some of my own poetry as an added bonus. There was no hassle doing it either; they built a ramp for the platform and the filming went really easily. It was one of my most enjoyable work experiences. The producer wrote to me afterwards and said, 'Well done, you did it magnificently. I'm very pleased with the results, hope you are too. Come again. Love Ralph.' I hope that this certainly will not be the only time that a disabled person gets space in the world of non-disabled-ghetto broadcasting.

13

'Hallelujah freedom, freedom way,
Hallelujah freedom, freedom day
Dr Hook

One aspect of my first theatre tour rooted itself deeply within me and gradually surfaced over the years. Our day in Edinburgh prison had really left an imprint in my mind, not only because of the atmosphere and the performance we did and the prison band we watched, but because I made a friend there. I realised that sometime, somehow, I definitely wanted to work in prisons. As with all aspirations, it was a while before I actually got the chance to go into prison as anything other than a friend of John's, but that friendship itself was good preparation for my later work.

John had chatted with me that day in Edinburgh and had quite overwhelmed me by giving me a painting he had done. Choked on emotion, I hadn't managed to verbalise my gratitude so I wrote to thank him for it. He replied and we became pen-friends. I never asked him his crime. He could have been a rapist for all I knew, but in a sense his crime was irrelevant. In his own way and in his own good time he told me what he did and what had got him into prison and I think that was probably the best way round. If I had pressed him it would have seemed like morbid curiosity. I wanted to practise what I preached, which is that we are all equal, so I accepted him as he was and he accepted me as I was. I think that our 'disabilities' were quite a good equaliser. I was in a wheelchair and he was in prison, the difference being that his prison was a trap and my wheelchair gave me freedom. However there was a vaguely subconscious feeling that we were both in our own kind of prison and at least I wasn't an able-bodied do-gooder. Many people used to ask me what crime he had committed and I would not say because it was irrelevant and it still is.

Our correspondence continued for a while and our letters revealed our sense of humour which is always a good point of contact.

What dumbfounded me was discovering that, out of all the people I was to meet in prison, John was a Christian. Since our lives were so different it was amazing to have such a major factor in common. He had been converted when he was sixteen in the Young Offenders and had been in prison ever since. We only found out that we were both Christians through a shared experience. He mentioned in one letter having just read 'a very moving story' called *Joni*, and he advised me to buy it because I would enjoy reading it. I was most touched by his words, 'She put her trust in Jesus and things really blossomed for her.' I wrote back saying I had read *Joni* and mentioned that I too was a Christian. John replied. 'Glad you enjoyed *Joni*, Ellen, it was great, she really did go through some pain. Reading it made me think of you and I had a feeling you would have went through most of her events, which weren't happy. You know this, it was good to read further down the page that you are a Christian. That's great, Ellen, I am a Christian myself but I must admit I don't really show it at times, but then again nobody's perfect.'

It is quite extraordinary how seemingly disparate aspects of life link up. *Joni* had meant an immense amount to me, and then a complete stranger who gave me a painting from his prison home turned out to have read *Joni* as well and to be a Christian.

In October 1982, which was just over a year after our correspondence began, John arranged for me to stay with

172

his parents in Glasgow so that I could meet him when he was allowed a brief glimpse of the outside world in the form of four hours' Special Escorted Leave (S.E.L.). Two of the four hours were allocated as travel time from Edinburgh to Glasgow. The plan was that I would stay over on Saturday night in readiness for John's visit on the Sunday but, unbeknown to me, the visit had been brought forward to the Saturday for some obscure prison reason. Due to train times from Bristol, the disastrous result was that I missed John completely. It was only by fifteen minutes. John's parents were extremely hospitable even though I had never met them before and I must have seemed thick because I only began to get to grips with their broad dialect shortly before I left.

Early in 1983, a second visit was arranged and John wrote saying, 'I asked them for an all nighter but they said "Nae chance".' Such was John's humour. This time I went to stay with his Bible study group leader, Neil, in Edinburgh so that I could travel with John to Glasgow and back in the car, giving us longer together. It amazes me now to think of it. Not only the fact that I had the energy to do it but boldness in going on my own to an unfamiliar place and my complete trust in my hosts and complete lack of fear. I wouldn't do it now, but I suppose I was stronger physically then. It wasn't such a big deal to spend the weekend with total strangers and trust them – and myself – to manage my various needs. Either you go for it and hope for the best and do things as you go along or you don't go at all.

I'm very glad I did it because everything went well except that I inadvertently got John into trouble. He had his next S.E.L. cancelled because of me, which made me feel terrible when I found out. First of all, I gave him two books. It turned out that this was prohibited because they were not declared beforehand. I simply copied his mother without realising that every gift has to be declared beforehand, like Customs. But not only that, I took a photograph of him outside the prison and again nobody told me that this was against regulations. This would have been all right if I hadn't sent John a copy of the photo. I was only recently told that the reason prisoners are not allowed photographs of the prison is in case they use it to work out an escape route. It would have helped if I had known at the time because John would not have been hauled up before the Governor and lost his privilege of leave.

It is a shame that the prison authorities could not have issued me with a duplicated list of 'do's' and 'don'ts'. I went on a course for prison visitors much later on and I cannot recall learning anything like that even then. Up until that time I had very little contact with the 'criminal world' and the police, and until you do, you don't realise the extent normal society runs on trust and the extent you expect to be trusted. Undeclared gifts could carry drugs, but because I would not use them for such a purpose I forgot that it was assumed by the prison authorities that I might. A word with me or a list of rules would have been much fairer to both of us than the summary denial of John's privileges. Considering a prison warder always escorts a prisoner outside, it would be more appropriate to reprimand or penalise the one in charge, but that sort of justice would not be in line with the 'system'!

It was not until years later that I wheedled the whole story out of John. At the time he merely mentioned his loss of S.E.L. It turned out that the prison had asked who took the photograph, which was rather silly because all mail is censored and I had sent the photos with a letter; it clearly was not Neil because he was in the photo too, so it could only have been me. But John refused to state the obvious or split on me and he replied that he didn't know. When I asked him why he did not give my name he told me that it just wasn't done. I was amazed that he never blamed me, but I think he was amazed at my questioning his loyalty.

The next visit was a surprise visit, which also wasn't allowed. I was up in Edinburgh for the Edinburgh Festival and had been told by a friend of John's that the

Education Officer could probably fix something up for me. John had been asked 'Are you expecting a visit?' which was a trick question because if he had said he was, they would think he had told me how to wangle it. He also wanted to give me a plant from the garden where he worked, but he couldn't risk asking because if had to reveal the reason all the other prisoners might want extra visits.

When they let me in they assumed I knew where I was going which was somewhat embarrassing. An officer took me into a dingy, tiny ante-room with just a dangling light bulb and I thought, 'Surely the visit won't be here!' Then I was taken into a larger room with several tables and a warder at one end. There were other people there too, and we had very little time as John had to be found and taken away from his work. We had to sit in a special way, as we weren't allowed to touch, although he put his foot on my wheelchair. He told me a great deal about prison conditions while his eyes darted around all the time. I took John another present which, again, wasn't officially allowed, but the officer was kind enough to let me give it to him when I explained it was a birthday present. It was Spandau Ballet's latest single. John had found out that I had a friend in the band and since he was a great fan he asked for a copy of their new single. I managed to get it signed by all the band which made it all the more special to John. Our time together was so short though, it was painful. I cried about that later. I also wrote a poem.

Prison Visit

Time
   like my emotions
       was
          running
            out

One hour
        was the prescribed dose
                of
                  sweet
                      medicine

Sixty minutes
        to exchange six hundred thoughts
                under
                      scrutinising
                              eyes

Longing
    to reach beyond the
                bars
                  of
                   time

Wanting
    to touch, hold, reassure
                yet
                  not
                    sure

Afraid
    a glance at my watch
                would
                    lose
                      time

Visits were always tough and after the next one I wrote to
Jim: 'I wish I could talk to you now. I've just visited John
in prison. I feel numbed. I wish I could cry to get it out of
my system but I can't . . . still, I got one and a half hours
with him. I'm lucky I got in to see him at all. I had very
negative feelings last night and this morning about the
visit. I knew by intuition there had been a breakdown in
the organisation of it. So it didn't surprise me when I got
to the prison and found the man who was supposed to
have made the arrangements wasn't there and had left no

message about me. I don't quite know who "authorised" my getting in. Just turning up at a prison and seeing the person you want to see is unheard of, but my friend, Ralph, pleaded for me and I used my feminine wiles and my disability in a subtle way. I'm aware that they don't know how to handle a woman in a wheelchair, or haven't learned that they are no different.' I would not normally do that but prison is a manipulative world and I did a little manipulation back. In any case, I had been assured the necessary arrangements were in hand. 'Actually it was funny Ralph being there because one of John's first comments was how pleased he was I hadn't got my hair wildly spikey like last time, and I pointed to Ralph saying "Here's the guy who cut it!" I never saw John turn so red so rapidly.'

Most of our communication was by letter although we had to be careful due to the censorship. I received one letter which avoided the normal scrutiny because it was a 'backdoor' letter, smuggled out of prison. It was written in an entirely different tone and gave a fascinating insight into prison life: 'Just remember this Ellen see, when you go to the prison for your visits don't let the nice talk from the screws make you think that life is like that all the time from them because see the minute you leave the building it's back to the old mean face. Off comes the false face they put on for the visitors I've seen it too many times. Just yesterday we had the inspector of prisons in, the top man, you know this Ellen all the prisoners they thought were going to complain to him were locked up until he went away.'

Ironically enough, when John was in a semi-open prison and I would have been allowed an all-day visit, I somehow never made it. He told me my visit would come under a 'welfare visit' category because of my disability. I was rather amused because I wasn't sure whose welfare. Was it mine or John's?

He came out in 1987 and came to stay with me in London that summer for a few days, the first time he had been away from Scotland. Like so many ex-prisoners it took him ages to find any work. He eventually did a government training scheme but then had to wait a fair while before he got any kind of job. The stigma keeps men in prison much longer than their sentences.

Visiting in prison did not put me off my original idea of working in that sphere. If anything, it only served to fan the flames. As a consequence I did a prison visiting course which was great fun even though I did not learn much more than I already knew. I also worked with 'Clean Break Theatre Company' on a play called *The Easter Egg* in 1985. It was a women's theatre company made up mainly of ex-prisoners. When I heard about them I rang them, explaining that I wasn't an ex-prisoner but in a sort of metaphorical prison, and that a great friend of mine was a prisoner. It was an able-bodied theatre company so I was thrilled that they were interested enough to employ me. Working with them combined my passions for theatre and prison. One part I played was a judge. I wore a vast academic gown which kept getting caught in my wheels and I had a huge wig which weighed me down. I must have looked hilarious when I came on stage. Even so, the actresses said the way I pronounced the sentence was chillingly close to the way sentence had once been pronounced over them.

While I was on the prison visiting course I met an education officer from Holloway prison who proved to be a useful contact later. In the autumn of 1987 I read about the poet Ken Smith, who had been writer in residence at Wormwood Scrubs for two years, and I thought, 'That's it. That's what I want to do.' It suddenly struck me that my work in prisons should be in the form of poetry workshops. I set about finding funding. I contacted the education officers of my two local prisons, Pentonville and Holloway. They welcomed my workshops, although the education officer at Pentonville was uncertain at first because many of the men were illiterate.

I was lucky enough to meet up with Ken Smith who was very helpful and gave me some good tips. He had got it into his head that I had been in prison as a criminal, so I joked about smuggling dope in my wheelchair after I had set him straight on the matter.

January 6th, 1988 was my first day. Although I was looking forward to it, part of me was terrified and wondered 'What on earth am I doing?' Amazingly, I had read that morning, 'I can do everything through him who gives me strength'. It calmed me down immensely.

Once I was inside Pentonville I sensed all eyes were on me, questioning what I was up to and why. I wanted to look and take everything in, but did not want to pry. It was impossible for me to merge into the background and, not for the first time, I wished I could become as small and unnoticeable as a fly on the wall. Even the classroom doors had glass panes; it was very distracting. There were eyes everywhere and every door had an eyehole. I was more aware of eyes than keys. The men had, quite rightly, not been told that I was disabled so I chatted a bit to put them at their ease.

Holloway had a completely different atmosphere. It was a modern building, light, had new, decent furniture, plants in the windows and was cleaner. The women wear their own clothes so it was difficult to tell who was staff and who was inmate in the education department. As I reached the department there was a long corridor with glass panels where they were painting a mural of a sea scene. Its beautiful design was vibrant with huge blue waves and brightly coloured leaping fish. It made a striking contrast to the drab brown brick walls and mostly bare corridors elsewhere in Holloway. I noted in my journal: 'It will be exciting to watch the mural grow each week as I go past.' The following week I wrote in my journal: 'Like a candle in a dungeon, the stained glass painting is the highlight of my "journey" through all the labyrinthine corridors and locked doors to the education department. Today two flying swans had appeared above the waves, beautifully painted and gracefully expressing freedom.'

Neither prison was ever predictable. My prison motto became: 'Always expect the unexpected'. My classes were small, but I had specified a maximum of ten. Once at Pentonville I had the remedial maths class in as well, which brought the numbers up to twelve and there weren't enough chairs. They got a bit rowdy then and wound each other up and I don't think I handled it very well. I found myself thinking, to what extent do I use discipline on men who are cooped up most of the day and probably need to let off steam in the relative freedom of my class? I didn't mind them chatting a bit among themselves so long as they got the work done. However I felt even less in control when one prisoner, Barry, knew more about Japanese poetry than I did. It was embarrassing and made me feel a fraud especially when another man said, 'Is it the first time you've taught poetry, then?'

It was very interesting to see the development in those who came every week. When Barry came to my first class he had never written poetry before, but by week four he had written an amazing poem about life, comparing it to climbing a mountain. Only when you reach the top do you feel 'hole'. The spellings were out of this world.

The women, unlike the men, were not afraid of showing their true emotions through poetry. One young woman wrote a lovely but sad poem about her seven-year-old daughter which made her cry. The same day, another woman was in tears and too distressed to work because she was awaiting trial and faced a possible sentence of seven years. She said to me, 'My brother phoned from America. He's thirty-two and he was in tears.' Sometimes I had to choke back the tears myself.

All of them found it easier to write romantic poetry or poetry on themes that expressed their frustration, desire for freedom and a new start in life. One of my regulars, Frank, a romantic at heart, wrote a poem inspired by a Canaletto from an art book I had taken in. 'Looking out dear old London, town . . . wearing a deep crimson gown.' He compared the sunset to a fire and described how it quenched his desire.

When we came to do comedy, neither the men nor the

180

women felt like writing comic material. Part of the problem for the men was that Pentonville made them feel totally lethargic; that day they were falling asleep and said they felt drugged. To add insult to injury, one man was fed up because the education department had lost his exercise book. 'I'm gutted,' he said. He took pride in the work he had done and it clearly epitomised to him the 'couldn't care less' attitude of prison. But on the same day, while the rest of the class only wanted to discuss parole, letters, censors and drugs, another prisoner, Aston, was quietly writing a brilliant, powerful poem with good use of rhythm and repetition. It was about a man with no job and no money and the last few lines went: 'He wasn't doing nothing, he was doing something, he was hanging, he was dead.' I persuaded him to read it out and the others clapped. It must have struck a chord.

A week before my last class in Pentonville, one of the teachers said they wanted me to continue. They had received enthusiastic feedback from the men and it had been a very popular class. When the men heard it was my last week they were dismayed, saying 'Why?', 'Got too famous for us then?', 'Not coming no more?' The workshops had been a success but, as ever, there were other pressing demands on my life. I very much wanted to carry on so was torn, but with my other commitments it proved impossible. I hope someone else took on from where I left off, for the prisoners' sake, and I hope it's not the last time I go to prison! I wrote up final thoughts in my prison journal – Pentonville, February 23rd: 'I smiled at the man serving tea as I went down the wing for the last time. It was a smile of solidarity but no one smiled back. I can't say that I blame them. I'm free to come and go as I please.'

Holloway, February 25th: 'As I left, I went past the glass-panelled mural. All the paint on several sections had been scraped off. Apart from looking drab and naked, it epitomised working in prison, i.e. three steps forward and two steps back. That's how I felt as I passed through the last door with a heavy heart. I don't regret my time there, far from it. But could I actually go back and face starting from scratch again?'

14

'She's running to stand still'
U2

A Speedy Disposal

He was destined to bring peace to the earth
but there would be too lowly a place for birth
and his mother was far too young
to cope with a burden of a son
so a speedy disposal was prescribed

He was to be the world's greatest teacher
not to mention carpenter and preacher
but his mother was not married
to the father of the child she carried
so a speedy disposal was prescribed

He was to become the ideal King
but not without ridicule or suffering
and his mother could not afford
to give him the upbringing of a Lord
so a speedy disposal was prescribed

His mother however was not led astray
by the professional pressures of her day
Respecting the seed that she hadn't planned
it grew into the greatest gift to man
as the speedy disposal was defied

'As I have a genetic disability (muscular dystrophy) I feel very strongly that babies should not be aborted, particularly if the only reason is because they are disabled, or "abnormal". Who is to play God and judge what the norm is?'

I wrote this in a letter on October 1st, 1987 to David Alton M.P. in support of his Private Member's Bill to reduce the upper time limit of abortion from twenty-eight to eighteen weeks after conception. My letter was sparked off by a television programme. Helena dragged me, wet and dripping, from the shower, to watch David Alton and his opponents debate the issue of abortion on the talk show hosted by Robert Kilroy-Silk. Part of the debate centred on the issue of abortion for unborn disabled babies. There was no exemption clause in David Alton's bill for children found to be disabled in the womb and this was the cause of some debate. The discovery of muscular dystrophy in an unborn child is now considered to be sufficient grounds for abortion without question.

Two things impressed me about the television programme: firstly, they did not have one single disabled person on the show to put forward their viewpoint. I felt very strongly that these able-bodied people had no right to represent disabled people. If they had been white people speaking on behalf of black people there would have been an outcry. The second thing that struck me was the composure of David Alton himself. He listened with gentle humility to his opponents and was far from your average ranting M.P. He put his case calmly and with reason against vehement opposition.

I sat down immediately and wrote my response. I partly wanted to counteract the inevitable hate-mail that David Alton would receive (or 'hate-male', as I joked to him) but I also offered to give a disabled person's point of view on future television programmes. I was honest about myself and my disability and said that you can never predict the potential of an unborn disabled baby.

I did not really expect much to come of it. Members of

Parliament receive thousands of letters a year and I thought mine would not be that significant but, within days, his office contacted me. One of David Alton's researchers later told me that my letter had come at just the right time and was a real morale booster. David Alton himself announced at a rally in my presence that it was the most moving and the most influential letter he had ever received, which I find hard to believe. I was quite overwhelmed by that reaction for he was a man who received mountains of mail, and more than ever in relation to the Abortion Bill. Their enthusiasm for my letter compensated for the fact that, for some weeks afterwards, David Alton thought I was called Ellen Willy. I found myself quoted as such in several cuttings and even introduced to someone from the *Guardian* as Ellen Willy before I managed to correct the situation. Fortunately I could see the funny side of it.

Even before I met David Alton I found myself in the anti-abortion campaign. The first telephone call from his office thanked me for my letter and asked me whether I would be willing to appear on *Split Screen* as part of the debate. I was, of course, but in fact that interview did not happen until the time of the second reading. Trying to get my opinion over on television and in the newspapers turned out to be as difficult as Sisyphus rolling his stone up a hill forever. They really did not want to hear what I had to say. Amusingly enough the *News of the World* was after me again, but the first such interview I actually did was for a press agency. Because of previous experiences, I was very wary of them. The man who rang me promised me that I would be able to change facts that were incorrectly stated. He then went on to ask whether I was blonde or brunette. I found his questions so ludicrous I'm afraid I took the mickey a bit, so when he said, 'Would it be an impediment to marriage?' (meaning of course, would my disability prohibit sex or marriage?), I said 'What? Being brunette?' When he came to read it back it wasn't quite so funny and as usual I had to make some corrections, including the fact that he implied I had received numerous offers of marriage. I have had a few but I didn't want to overstate the case.

There was an uncredited reference to me in the *Guardian* but the editor of *Disability Now* guessed that it was me and commissioned me to write an article on abortion and disability. This was my first paid work as a journalist apart from odd book reviews. I wasn't at all sure I could do it, but I thought I could give it a shot, since the subject was so close to my heart, and I surprised myself. I have the campaign to thank for giving me the confidence to write, paving the way to more regular work in journalism. On October 13th I met David Alton, and was filmed with him in an interview for *Weekend World*. As usual, we spent ages hanging around waiting to be filmed and then we did a solid interview. There were murmurs of 'powerful stuff', and the whole thing was watered down to part of one sentence of mine. There was a shot of me in conversation with David Alton while somebody narrated over the film. I think I said something like, 'I've outlived the doctors' expectations . . .' (fade . . .) In other words, don't blink or you will miss me.

Much the same thing happened with *This Week Next Week*. My lengthy interview with David Alton was completely cut, although they did use a brief clip of me arriving at the House of Commons and saying 'Oh, yes' to David Alton's chat on Simon de Montfort. It all looked innocuously like 'cripple's day out' rather than showing that disabled people can have political opinions. David Alton was clearly disappointed, saying in the studio interview, 'But if we could have seen what Ellen Wilkie had to say . . .' He was swiftly cut by the presenter.

The whole point of my involvement in the campaign was to allow disabled people to have an authentic voice rather than for David, as an able-bodied person, to try to represent disabled people. Now, I decided to take a little of the media campaign into my own hands. My journalist friend, Martin Wroe, advised me to ring the health editor of the *Independent* proposing I put the disability aspect across in an article for them. After all, having written one article for *Disability Now*, why not the nationals? But the response was equally squashing. According to the editor there was not enough to fill an article by a disabled person who was anti-abortion and he tried bringing in red herrings like, 'Children are nothing without their parents.' He attempted to make me contradict myself by asking me all sorts of tricky questions such as did I oppose abortion on the grounds of disability at earlier stages of pregnancy? I pointed out that it would be inconsistent not to, but disability is not a contentious issue in the early stages of pregnancy because the tests are not available.

In any case, the Alton bill was merely concerned with reduction in the upper limit for an abortion, because a baby killed at twenty-eight weeks, or even earlier, could be a viable child if it were a premature birth. There was no disability exemption clause in the bill but one of the compromises being asked for was to allow abortion on grounds of disability to continue up to twenty-eight weeks. Naturally, I don't believe any disabled baby should be aborted because that is discrimination. Abortion for me is a human rights issue and in line with the United Nations' Declaration on Human Rights. Everyone has the right to life, disabled or not. There are thousands of babies with disabilities who have been aborted, and muscular dystrophy is one of the most common disabilities. Moreover, I am not exceptional in confounding the gloomy medical predictions.

The national newspapers may not have embraced my opinion on disability but four able-bodied women journalists, all of whom were in favour of abortion on the grounds of disability, were given an outlet. I wrote a letter to the *Guardian* about the insulting way Polly Toynbee referred to disabled people, using words like 'handicapped' and 'abnormal'. This simply underlined her ignorance of the subject. Disabled people do not consider themselves abnormal. Not so very long ago it was not 'normal' for women to be journalists. The sort of language used in relation to disability throughout the campaign set the disability movement back years. As for our 'suffering' or being 'victims' of our 'handicaps', there are plenty of able-bodied people who are miserable. Such things as suffering vary from individual to individual, depending on their frame of mind as well as their physical capabilities. If the fact that we might be miserable were grounds for abortion then, no doubt, we would all be dead. I even heard a doctor say on television that it would be better for society if disabled babies were not born. Doctors and midwives who refuse to perform abortions can lose their jobs. Such is the sad travesty of the Hippocratic oath. I ought to point out that it has never been illegal to terminate a pregnancy if the mother's health is at risk.

Not every single disabled person agrees with my view on abortion. Shortly after the bill had failed, I did a cabaret performance at an arts venue for disabled people. Halfway through my performance the compère stopped the show for a woman to interview me. She included some questions on abortion. They had advertised the interview before asking me whether I would do it. I would not have agreed to it otherwise but, presented with a *fait accompli*, I was too kind for my own good. I certainly regret my decision and when the night arrived, the last thing I felt like was being quizzed on my career. The interviewer had not got all her facts right either and said, 'You're a member of S.P.U.C. (Society for the Protection of the Unborn Child), aren't you?' She was implying that I was therefore right wing. The very reason I chose not to belong to any such group was to avoid categorisation. When she went on to tell me I was not very involved in the disability movement I pointed out that, on the contrary, my involvement with the movement was inextricably interwoven with my ideas on abortion because I did not see how anyone could be part of the disability movement and advocate abortion on the grounds of disability. If I joined any pro-life group it would be Feminists Against Eugenic Practices because that is very much the angle I find congenial. It would not harm any pro-abortion feminist to look at the opposing opinions within their movement.

I finally got some sort of a breakthrough in the media with my appearance on *News at Ten*. I was telephoned by the I.T.N. office and I told the producer that I was a professional working woman and twice so far my time had been almost completely wasted as I had been cut. 'Don't misunderstand me,' I said. 'I would be very happy to do it, but if you really don't want my opinion then don't ask for it.' I knew there was no guarantee I would not be cut, but at least they could give it some thought before wasting my time. They assured me they did want me and kept their word. I even received a massive bouquet of flowers for my pains. Not only that – they used part of my poem 'Therapeutic Termination'.

Therapeutic Termination

We are the ones
who were to you
nothing to lose
we are the ones
who gave our lives
for your freedom to choose
we are the ones
who forgot all rights
we are the ones
deprived of a chance to fight
we are the ones
who never became your sons
we are the ones
who were silently slaughtered
before we became daughters
we are the ones
cut out in the prime
(but where do you draw the line?)
                     of life

> though voiceless
> you will hear us
> though powerless
> we will triumph
>
> outside time
> in another place
> we join the ranks
> for confrontation face to face
>
> we are the ones
> who stand before you
> and demand
> a life before death

The filming by the *News at Ten* crew taught me something new to be wary of. They came to my flat to film me *in situ* and, being so familiar with my surroundings, it didn't occur to me that a film crew might distort reality. I had forgotten about the holy quotes stuck on my bedroom wall. These quotes are all in one place above my desk so that when I am working I can use them as a source of strength if need be. Unfortunately they did look slightly over-the-top to the I.T.N. news crew and I could hear them whispering about filming them. They were things like 'Love is . . .' and 'God, grant me the courage to change the things I can change, the serenity to accept the things I can't change and the wisdom to know the difference.' Once the crew saw them I was in a bit of a quandary. I had seen the way the media portrayed David Alton as a hardline Roman Catholic with a fundamentalist belief in the sanctity of life. They tended to film in front of cathedrals to compound that religious image, which falsely represents his motivation and is calculated to undermine his credibility. It is another common fallacy for pro-abortionists to assume that all anti-abortionists are politically right wing. The filming of my holy quotes was aimed to make me look like a right wing fundamentalist and I am neither. However, I thought that if I asked them not to film them, it would make me look as if I was ashamed of them, so I let them carry on. It was only later that I had a little chuckle to myself as I realised the irony of their picking on 'God, grant me the courage to change the things I can . . .' in the context of the campaign, which was probably a subtlety beyond the eyes of the film crew. Helen, who was working for me, was furious at their stereotyping of me. 'Why didn't they go and film in the bathroom and show your pictures of nude women?' she said.

By the time it came to the second reading of the bill the *Today* programme on B.B.C. Radio 4 asked to interview me. I told them I wasn't interested in answering questions any more but that I had certain statements I would like the opportunity to make. Even then you are not in control of the way they edit, and their version of what I said was very emasculated.

When another television programme opted for an able-bodied woman with a wishy-washy opinion on disability to give the disability perspective on abortion I wrote a poem and sent it to the producer.

Stifled Voices

cry for our world
cry for our world
I cry for our world
where white speaks for black
and non-disabled for disabled
where the perfect planned and privileged
are liked, loved and worshipped
and alone have the right to life
where ignorance breeds ignorance
and fear breeds fear
and power is snatched from those who know
where fools make the decisions
and lay down the law for us all
and take choice from the oppressed blow by
 blow

cry for our world
cry for our world
I cry for our world
but my voice is only one drop in the ocean of
    messages
and how far can that reach without
    drowning
I don't know

It was not sour grapes that they hadn't chosen me, it was distress at the blatant discrimination, as if the media had already censored the viewers' opinions.

About a year later I was asked to do a one-minute soapbox on abortion. One minute? I nearly fell out of my chair in disbelief. What I have to say would take at least one hour. Condensing my thought so extremely was a well-nigh impossible demand. It may have been a one-minute slot but at least I knew my performance would not be tampered with or my words edited after filming.

The more I became involved in the campaign, the more I realised how anti-social it is considered to be pro-life. A great many people who have had abortions don't want to hear that it is murder and others probably convince themselves it is not. Those who have aborted disabled babies don't want to hear that those babies could have had successful and viable lives. I am not unaware of the social implications of no abortion. Society needs to provide better education so that there are fewer unwanted pregnancies, and a great deal more support for single parents, particularly mothers. Better support should also be provided for disabled people, so the pressures of living in society with a disability do not amount to the disabled person being handicapped, but rather allow him or her to lead a normal life. If a child really is unwanted then there is always the possibility of adoption. Today there are more couples waiting for disabled babies than there are babies available to adopt, quite apart from the shortage of able-bodied babies. The mental difficulties involved in adoption should not be belittled, but neither should the physical risks or the mental scarring, involved in abortion.

I have a lot to say on the subject and most of my opinions were stated in my contribution to David Alton's book *Whose Choice Anyway?* published by Marshall Pickering. In that book I was, at last, given the space to make my point. Before that, the little air-time I had been granted produced a watered-down version of what I believed. As a result any media implications that disabled people were used as human footballs by pro-lifers during the campaign were highly objectionable. If anything, the media were using us as footballs and not only people with disabilities received the kicks. David Alton was as much a victim himself. Such inferences were insulting to disabled people who chose to give up their time to support a political cause they believed in.

To abort someone on the grounds of disability is the first step on a very slippery slope. It opens the door to eugenic practices and there are many in our society who are eugenists quite unashamedly. If it is disabled babies today it will be babies with A.I.D.S. tomorrow. This is not ludicrous scaremongering. At what precise point does the eugenic theory stop? No one can protect a child from accidents and if it then becomes disabled is it to forfeit its life? Even now it is considered anti-social for a mother to go ahead and have a disabled baby when she knows it is disabled. Such a baby is regarded as a drain on society's resources, but many disabled people contribute far more to society than the average able-bodied football hooligan. Should we get rid of potential football hooligans in the womb or abort babies on the possibility of a mental illness they might develop later in life, like schizophrenia? Even now babies are being aborted on suspicion of spina bifida or muscular dystrophy because the tests are not foolproof and may give a false indication. In other words, able-bodied babies are being aborted by 'accident', but mothers cannot simply go out and get another product, like a jar of coffee from the supermarket. No one can predict how any child is going to turn out but once it is conceived it has the right to find out for itself. At the risk of sounding like a messenger of doom, only recently I read articles suggesting that any women refusing to have amniocentesis or similar tests for disability during pregnancy, or refusing to have abortions when they know their babies are disabled, should be denied the right to any state help in bringing up the child. Pro-life supporters may be accused of being right wing but doesn't that sound rather fascist to you?

Justice Anthem

You may have your say today
but justice will have the final say
justice has a strange old way
of turning up trumps
in unexpected time or place

Cowards will use trickery
to keep injustice as it stands
while some claim they fight for human rights
but fail to see
their glaring inconsistency

Neutralists in fact support
through their lack of opposition
those who sit upon the fence
adopt their selfish ploy
to keep their comfortable position

Some may have their way today
but justice will sweep all before her
justice has a strange old way
of claiming the victory
in unexpected time or place

15

'maybe you and he will not agree
but you need him to show you new ways to see'
Bruce Cockburn

Maybe the poet is gay
but he'll be heard anyway

Maybe the poet is drugged
but he won't stay under the rug

Maybe the voice of the spirit
in which case you'd better hear it

Maybe he's a woman
who can touch you where you're human

Male female slave or free
peaceful or disorderly

Maybe you and he will not agree
but you need him to show you new ways to see

Bruce Cockburn – Toronto, January 1982

I remember visiting Granny Wilkie once when I was a child. She was very old by then and quite ill. She was confined to bed and, unaware how ill she was, decided she wanted to go for a walk. 'Where are my shoes, John?'

195

she said to my father, and I sat and watched while my parents and brothers hunted for the shoes. It was a pretence, for she was not well enough to go out but nobody wanted to say that to her. However, neither I nor Alcuin realised how ill she was so when Alcuin found the shoes and announced, 'Here they are!' he was immediately hushed up and I was shocked that my parents were deceiving my Granny in that way. I could not see why she shouldn't go for a walk. Years later, I understood how ill she was but the incident is vividly imprinted on my memory as an illustration of how I am often forced to sit, observe and reflect rather than actively participate in what others are doing around me, especially when I'm out of my flat or electric wheelchair. I think that's partly why I am a poet.

In other words, much of my poetry stems from being sedentary which is due to my disability. I have a keen eye and an ability to pick up on every minute detail in people and life that others would never notice. Helena refers to it as my antennae. It can be an annoying streak as people can't get away with anything. For example, at parties I sit and watch the physical dynamics taking place and how people react to each other. That's not to say that I'm a wallflower and that people don't chat to me or I to them, but I don't immediately get pounced on as a 'bit of fluff' – thank goodness – and if people have nothing of interest to communicate, I prefer to observe.

At any public occasion where I can't take my electric wheelchair I have to wait for people to come and talk to me, so while I am waiting I find it amusing to take in human behaviour. Poetry is also an economic form of writing and this too may have influenced my choice in writing poetry rather than prose. Who's to say it would or wouldn't have developed if I hadn't had a disability? Even when I was as young as eight, my English teacher wrote on my report, 'She has a keen sense of rhythm and much enjoys writing poetry.' If I did not possess some innate poetic talent maybe it would have been fine art and, indeed, my school report for art at the age of eleven mentioned my 'Rich, original work'. I nearly did art 'A' Level. But due to the precise nature of my disability my poetic streak was enhanced, I believe. Having said that, I am convinced that if I had been able-bodied I would also have done something artistic.

I always think of the starting point of my 'poetic career' as, at age fourteen, the time I won a poetry competition. I had to write an original psalm. I have always found the Psalms comforting. Their writers seem to have so much in common with me. When I read the Psalms the Bible becomes a present day reality. I once underlined part of Psalm 31 in thick black pen because I particularly related to it at the time. Psalm 31:10 says 'For my life is spent with sorrow, and my years with sighing; my strength fails because of my misery, and my bones waste away' (Revised Standard Version). All very sombre. My little contribution to that genre won the competition and, a few years later, I went on to win another one held by the Upstream Theatre Club in Waterloo. We had to incorporate within the poem six titles from their previous productions and that made it difficult to avoid it sounding stilted. We were also given the added restriction of only three topics to choose from. I chose 'Christmas in the Highlands'.

Christmas in the Highlands

I recollect
the wind ravening over the lochs and pines
like the lion in winter
thunder wrenching the heavens apart
snow transforming the crofts into white mausoleums

I will not forget
the tree that woke up
to my little sister's touch
as she clothed it in starbright decoration
the promise she made to reawaken it next year

the lights are dazzling yet
though all outside is barren
how I long for Easter
when all living things are born
and birds sing their anthology at dawn

The first major flow of poems came when I had left school and university and was going through my 'blue' period. I was in tears most days and poured out my sorrows to Jim. Until I leafed through my old diaries I had forgotten how terrible it was at that time. Jim was the first person I talked to so deeply about my life and poetry and Christianity. I learned a lot about Christianity through his making me look at things more critically, but not in a negative manner. The poetry stemmed from feelings of isolation, depression and loneliness. I didn't have many friends in Bristol because virtually all of my university friends had gone. I started writing very sombre poems about intense feelings including love and loneliness. In one poem, 'The Hill', I saw life as an uphill struggle. It ended by saying, 'my friends I'm sorry I've fallen to the ground' because I had no tufts of security to hold on to. It was probably not something Shakespeare would have been proud of but I suppose it expressed my feelings at the time. My 'down' state went on for months and months. I had days when I was fine but generally I was depressed. Friends of mine said later that at the time they thought I was heading for a nervous breakdown. Perhaps if I hadn't cried so much and expressed my sorrow verbally and through poetry I would have cracked. Who knows? Maybe if I hadn't been a Christian I would have crumbled. I am not saying that Christians are immune from breakdowns or that having one is a chink in your Christian armour. That would be insulting to Christians who go through the experience. But I feel that for me personally my Christianity kept me strong.

At first I didn't really want to show my poems to anyone but I continued to write them. That's when the songs came along because Jim put some of them to music.

He raved over my lyrics and encouraged me to write more songs. He once said, 'If you keep on writing lyrics like that you'll make thousands of pounds per year.' I replied, 'I'd love to. I didn't know I'd be good enough.' Quite a bit of my early poetry is embarrassing to look back on, though I realise if I hadn't written it then my poetry would never have developed to what it is now. I didn't have any training nor did I particularly want to read anybody else's poetry, because then nobody could accuse me of plagiarism or copying a certain poet's style. I wanted my own original style, although it is impossible for any artist to be completely free of influences. You cannot become Shakespeare overnight. The more you write, the more you do develop your own style.

A fairly major influence must have been my classical training. Some classical writing, particularly Greek tragedy and lyric poetry, is so condensed that you have painstakingly to fill in the meaning. This must have slipped into my subconscious and contributed to forming my own economic style. Interestingly, in 1984, the poet Stewart Henderson commented in a letter, 'You've managed to take an experience and subject it to the restraints of disciplined word economy. Something that very few poets achieve.'

As my career developed, I started to perform my poems in shows. The first ones I did were in Graeae productions, *Casting Out* followed by *A Cocktail Cabaret* in 1984 which we opened at the Edinburgh Festival before a three-week London run. I also wrote some songs for the cabaret and performed them live professionally for the first time. I was in my element.

After *A Cocktail Cabaret* I wanted to perform more poetry. There was an Arts Centre Group festival on that autumn and I noticed some poets were down to perform their work and that gave me the idea to offer my services. I was accepted, and excited at the prospect. I didn't know where to start but I knew this was what I wanted to do and felt the A.C.G. was a safe environment for my first gig. Even so, I was a bundle of nerves and wrote a poem as a springboard to my first performance. It later appeared in my book *Pithy Poems*.

Poetry Reading

What if I don't start in the right way?
What if they don't like what I have to say?
What if they stand up and walk away?
What if they don't feel edified anyway?
Will they applaud nicely, smile politely and thank me
through embarrassed eyes?

Will they think me simple?
Will they think me obscure?
Will they form a definite opinion of me?
Or will they be left unsure?
Will they even think me a downright bore?

What if they get my name wrong on the programme?
And nobody knows who I am?
Will they be disappointed that I have no books to
sign?
Am I not more than a neurotic artistic bohemian
thespian?
Do I ask too many questions?

What if I don't bother to get out of bed and do it
today?

I had seen Roger McGough perform his poetry when we were touring with Graeae and if I have been influenced by anyone it's him and Brian Patten. In fact I did my first public reading ever in Brian Patten's presence on Radio One's *Studio B15*. I later bumped into him at the Edinburgh Festival and kept in touch in a very tenuous way. He was really instrumental in my daring to branch out and 'go public' by sending poems off for publication. In order to judge the true worth of my poems I felt I needed the honest opinion of a respected poet, rather than a

200

friend I respected. So I sent a selection of poems for his perusal and he was gracious enough to reply saying, 'Lots of these are really worth keeping/publishing and I hope things work out that way.' I was genuinely taken aback but obviously very pleased and from then on I had the confidence and knowledge that generally my poetry was of a professional standard.

I was a member of the Poetry Society for a number of years before I finally stopped subscribing in 1989 because I didn't want to support or contribute to perpetuating their elitist attitude. At least it gave me inspiration for a poem entitled 'A.M.' which stands for ante-meridian of course, but my title is also an esoteric abbreviation for anti-metre.

A.M.

in the blur of waking
my thoughts and notions
are floating round the room
in various levitating motions
only to be swept away
by nimble-fingered Day
insisting they surrender to her broom
commanding 'Hush'
with dustpan and brush
as she draws back Heaven's curtains.

my ideas sculpt their own metre
rejecting the rigour of earth-created norm
they tap their own rhythm, their own rhyme
in a dance of newly-invented time
they chorus an anthem at dawn
as fledgling verse is born

In 1982 I had started getting the Greenbelt Festival magazine *Strait* and I particularly noted their poetry page. I read it and thought, 'Well, mine's as good as this. Perhaps I can get my poetry published.' *Stride* and *Doors* were the first poetry magazines to publish my work. Up until then my work had been restricted to disability magazines.

1982 was also the year I went to Austria for a holiday. One day, while other people were rushing round the Prater, the permanent funfair outside Vienna, I quietly sat and took in the human behaviour around me. These observations formed themselves into a poem and I committed it to paper.

Prater

> high sky-diving dipper
> colours whirling round
> to the ground
> up and down
> sickly sweet greasy smells
> mouth-melting spun sugar-white floss
> rip-off chips and burgers gobbled greedily
> coke cans gulped thirstily
> sample the beer-garden's hot shade
> must spend a '3 schillings' quickly
> shrieks squeals delight
> dread and apprehension
> gripping tension
> I'm dizzizzizzy spinning
> letet me
> STOP

Not long after that I went to the poets' group at the A.C.G. The evening was led by another poet, Evangeline Paterson. It was my first meeting and I hadn't realised we were supposed to bring our poems to read and discuss. I happened to have my diary with me in which I had written my poem about the funfair. I was very hesitant to read it out as it was unfinished but Evangeline was impressed and told me to finish it off and send it to her. She wrote back a very encouraging letter telling me I had a way with words and that I should carry on writing.

Sometimes it was a process I could hardly hold back, as I pointed out in a letter to Jim in February 1985: 'Recently I've been writing virtually a poem a day. I have to do it. It's almost an instinct like eating or going to the loo.'

By this time I'd had a reasonable quantity of poems published in various magazines. After a while the thrill palled, and I no longer wanted my work to be restricted to magazine readership. I sent a selection of poems to various publishers but I was gradually coming round to the idea that I would have to be my own publisher. Many poets are the first time round, in order to gain credibility.

Early in 1985 I saw an advert in *Strait* asking for people to perform at the Methodist Association of Youth Clubs which gathers annually at the Westminster Central Hall in London. I was neither Methodist nor a youth, nor was I that old, so I got the booking and they commissioned me to write a poem on their theme 'Life Begins'. It was a really lively atmosphere which I love for performing. However, when I was doing my sound check before the show, the technician not so tactfully suggested that perhaps I should read only one poem. He evidently had no confidence in my ability to hold the attention of a young audience for more than a minute, judging from his comments about the rowdy audience. I told him in no uncertain terms that if my poetry was not good enough then I would accept the consequences. One girl came up to me and said she wished she were studying my poetry for 'O' Level because then she would understand it. As it happened, I sold over a hundred copies of my poems (at a reduced rate as the buyers were mostly of school age). The majority wanted them signed so by the time I got to the last signature my arm had nearly dropped off and I don't suppose it was legible either – that's my signature, not my arm!

The M.A.Y.C. were the last impetus I needed to get the book published for they had said the kids really liked something to go away with and would buy it. I leapt into action and engaged the help of a graphic designer friend, Giles Davies. Although the first edition was a rush job and I put some poems in which I now cringe over, it sold out. I even had some good reviews.

When I published the second edition I improved the cover, added a photo, a biography and a contents page. After that a local group, Angel Arts, published four poems in their anthology and Virago expressed an interest at one stage. Greenbelt publications accepted my second collection, *Taboo Topic*, and I have plans and poems for several more. However, getting poetry published is 'like throwing a rose petal over a cliff and waiting for the echo' to quote a poet overheard talking to another poet and passed on to me via a letter from a man who bought a copy of *Pithy Poems*. In my frustration over publishing I wrote a poem one day called 'Publishing Sea'.

Publishing Sea

endlessly swimming in a surfeit of sea
forcing my head above the surface constantly
fighting not to drown in the welling waves
wondering if there will come a time when I am saved
picked out by some lifeguard who can see
though from afar that there is some worth in me
taken back to the surf to play in safety

In October 1986 I wrote to Nic, 'I very much want to pursue my career as a poet and thus a performer of my own work.' While I have developed my poetry over the years, I have also, gradually, worked at my singing and poetry performances. I love the variety, the freedom and the control over my own material. I have always been a lover of music. I loved listening to Andrew playing, as the notes floated up to my attic room, and I taught myself to play the piano from Andrew's first piano books. I was influenced by his musical tastes in my teens, e.g. Simon and Garfunkel, The Incredible String Band, Loudon Wainwright III. I had a piano teacher for a while but she coughed smokey breath all over me and grabbed my hands saying, 'Not like that, but like this,' and then she would take over completely. I disliked her so much I did little, but just before I gave up piano lessons at the age of fourteen my teacher wrote on my report, 'Ellen works well at her pieces and technical exercises. She takes an interest in musical format and her aural response is good.' It's a shame I stopped really because I had played Bach in the school concert when I was eleven.

Some people still haven't caught on to the fact that I am a singer but I have always sung in shows since 1981. I wrote to Jim while I was on tour that year, 'I felt happiest on Friday when I was singing as a warm-up. It was strange, I suddenly felt this was what I ought to be doing. I'm not gifted with a good enough voice to sing professionally but at the moment I wish I was. I'm sure it is only a passing thing, the next time you see me I'll probably have forgotten all about it. Let's hope so.' Interestingly, my teacher had written on my report when I was eight, 'Ellen sings tunefully.' But Jim was the first person whose judgment I trusted who told me to my face, 'Your voice is really good.' That gave me confidence.

After my singing in tours with Graeae I found that many people were complimenting me on my voice. One woman even said it reminded her of Joni Mitchell's. Some asked me whether I had had my voice trained. I hadn't at the time but the comment made me think I could perhaps improve it vastly with a bit of training. Consequently I took up singing lessons and made some progress. One musician friend said my voice was astral. Astral? Perhaps he meant it would make the stars fall. My present guitarist compared my vocal sound to Maddy Prior, of Steeleye Span, which I found highly flattering as I am a great admirer of hers. I feel certain I would sing better if it weren't for my posture but I comfort myself with a student's comment, made after a gig, that my voice was 'quite remarkable'.

Once I had got some training and been told that I did have 'a good enough voice to sing professionally', I was even more keen to branch out as a singer. But it was a long, hard struggle finding someone to accompany me. I did perform with Jim once in Covent Garden (market) and it was well received, but he went abroad to work.

When I had got my first copy of *Strait*, the Greenbelt magazine, back in 1982 I answered an advertisement for a singer in a band. Someone rang to find out more about me and I said I was in a wheelchair. They said that if it had been on personality I would have got the job straight away but they needed someone who could dance. How odd, I thought they were looking for a singer. After that I didn't reply to any more advertisements.

Image is disproportionately important these days. If you are performing poetry you can just about get away with it but singing is too image conscious. *Top of the Pops* is very little to do with vocal talent. I could compete with most of the singers on that programme; even well-established and respected singers do not necessarily have strong or attractive voices.

I decided to go it alone and put an advertisement on the A.C.G. noticeboard for a guitarist. I was by the front door waiting for my taxi to arrive and a man standing nearby offered to help me into the taxi. There was only one reply to the advertisement and it was the same man. He had already shown some awareness of disability and obviously was not fazed at the thought of a musical duo with me.

Musicians are a notoriously unreliable crowd and I've had to put up with some complete wallies who promise you the earth and praise your vocal and lyrical ability to the skies, then fail to turn up. The more reliable musicians tend to lack talent. Michael, my present guitarist, is brilliant and a talented composer too, but he has a full time job with the *London Review of Books* so cannot come on tour with me. That means I have to take a backing tape or else stick to poetry. Actually Michael is very committed to our duo 'Wilkie and the Tallboy' and wants to expand it. We would like sax, drums, keyboards . . . He has never once missed a rehearsal and he restored my confidence after various misfortunes. It's to his credit that I am singing now.

The first guitarist loved my material and I enjoyed his but he didn't take it that seriously. It was more of a hobby to him and he didn't mind if we mucked up a performance but I was trying to do it professionally. Once we did a shoddy set because we hadn't rehearsed enough and that destroyed my confidence. I just decided I wasn't capable of singing and clammed up for years. Disabled performers cannot afford to make mistakes because then we are patronised and people say, 'Aah – isn't it nice – considering . . .' We actually have to be better than able-bodied artists before we can be treated as equals.

Audience response is varied. Sometimes they're very quiet and I think, 'Oh my goodness. I've sent them off to sleep.' Other times I have to keep my cool and not laugh when I hear loud comments. I remember one man bopping away in front of me, more than a little drunk no doubt, who wrote a very touching poem for me. On another night I teased one of my audience at my own expense. The poster advertising my performance had called me a T.V. star but a man sat down next to me, blissfully unaware of the fact and asked me whether I was looking forward to the entertainment. I said: 'This Ellie Wilkie, well it says she's a T.V. star but she can't be if we don't know who she is.' He agreed. I wonder what he thought when he saw me perform.

One of my favourite poems, which goes down well with audiences of any age, is 'Who?'. When I performed it in the Iona Community the restless teenage lads suddenly paid attention, or so I was informed later.

Who?

Who put the bounce in a baby?
Who put the heat in fire?
Who put the beat in reggae?
And who put the burn in desire?

Who put the speed in wind?
Who put the crack in a whip?
Who put the sing in a spinning top?
And who put the wet in a drip?

Who put the comfort in a teddy?
Who put the scent in a flower?
Who put the peace in the colour green?
And who put the coolness in an April shower?

Who put the smoothness in glass?
Who put the cheek in a grin?
And who put the thrill in touch?
I would like to meet her or him.

I do find I get labelled when I am invited to festivals. I get booked for a lot of disability festivals or the disability section of festivals, or I get used because I am a woman. I'm glad of the work but it would be good to be booked on the strength of my poetry and nothing else, not my femininity, disability or Christianity. I don't want to be purely sub-culture. I don't yet turn down bookings because I value the experience but at the same time I want to be out in the big bad world. The one ambition I have left in life is to make an album. Michael's music and our songs generally deserve it. A cassette of poetry would be fun too. I have achieved all the things I thought I couldn't but wanted to do, apart from an album. A lot of people think I should and some assume I have already and others are wanting to buy it but no one is offering to produce it. Judging from poetry sales our album would sell well at gigs.

One gig I did as part of the Bradford Festival – in the disability slot, of course. The sound engineer didn't have the balance right so my backing tape drowned out my lyrics, which was annoying. Luckily I was blithely unaware of it because I was nervous at using a backing-track for the first time. So I was ultra-taken aback when some young lads came up to me afterwards and said they really enjoyed my spot. Now, young lads mean what they say. Their parting shot was 'See you on *Top of the Pops*.' Well, why not?

16

'I'm under the mercy and I'm O.K.'
Bruce Cockburn

'I never thought all those years ago in Bristol that you would have created the life that you have. When I used to visit you at home I felt despairing because I thought that your life would be burned up in those four walls in your parents' house. That you would be a burden to them and hate yourself . . . you have guts and I can't help but admire and love you for it. I wish I had a tenth of your strength and will-power . . .' An old university friend wrote that to me about eighteen months after I had moved to London.

Our word 'dynamite' is a derivative of the ancient Greek word 'dunamis' which contains several meanings including power and strength. A friend once wrote me a poem which contained the lines:

> You are a contradiction in terms
> So small, yet so powerful
> So helpless, yet so in control
> So dependent, yet so free.

Similarly, I would echo Paul in 2 Corinthians 10: 'The trouble with you is that you look at me and I seem weak and powerless, but you don't look beneath the surface.' I would like to think that, as with Paul in 2 Corinthians 4, 'Everyone can see that the glorious power within must be from God and is not our own' (Living Bible). Sometimes I am so explosive after suppressing anger with petty bureaucrats or patronising officials that I doubt my response appears very 'holy' at all. In a battle with British Rail in 1989 my patience was worn down until like a jack-in-the-box there was no holding me back. I do not enjoy being angry, but sadly it is sometimes the only way disabled people are taken seriously. It certainly produced the table I required on my train journey, though it was not a bloodless battle. I was constantly called 'my dear', told all the future plans of British Rail to help disabled people (which was not going to help me now) and asked why I didn't have a table attached to my wheelchair. Are businessmen asked why they don't have tables attached to their briefcases? I was told I 'couldn't possibly' fit in the space if I had a British Rail table in front of me and when I pointed out that I had done so many times previously I was told 'You can't have.' My frustration knew no bounds. I said if I were Maggie Thatcher, Bob Dylan or the Queen there would be a table in a flash, but because I was considered a nonentity they wouldn't do it. I also informed the British Rail representative that I had assisted with a report for the English Tourist Board and recommended a movable table. We can put men on the moon but British Rail, who made £3 million profit in 1988, cannot even provide an adjustable table for someone who pays the same price as any other Railcard holder.

I only wanted to make my journey with the same facilities available to me as anyone else, but it exhausted an inordinate amount of time and energy. It is this sort of unnecessary waste which produced the following entry in my diary on March 21st, 1988: 'I'm so tired. I'm tired of being tired. Tired of not being able to stop without worrying about having to run twice as fast to catch up, thereby making myself twice as tired . . . and on . . . and on . . . Tired of falling short of the mark, of trying to live up to people's contradictory expectations, tired of being a famous nobody. Tired of being drained for no personal gain due to my "fame" while this fame is denied at others' convenience. Tired of my female vulnerability, tired of exploitation, tired of trying not to be tired, tired of exhausting myself with trying, tired of pretending, tired of protecting other people from my tiredness, tired of producing imaginary energy, tired of proving, tired of daily life.'

Not long after that, I was buoyed up by reading: 'He personally will come and pick you up and set you firmly in place, and make you stronger than ever' (1 Peter 5:10, Living Bible). It's a pity I had not 'chanced' upon that before when I had written in a similar vein to Nic in October 1986: 'I can't work under pressure. I just crumble in an exhausted heap. Coping with daily domestic living is all I can handle sometimes . . . I'm realising my limitations and don't intend to apologise for not being able to keep up in the rat-race!! I do have ambitions but they have to be long-term.'

Conversation with a Body

Don't let me down
I've not finished yet
You've done me proud
It's been a strong companionship
You're finding it a bind
and straining at the leash
but I've designed dreams in my mind
that I want to see released
You've done far more
than you were guaranteed to do
It's a great love affair
and I want the best for you
so hold on for me
wait until I'm through
don't back out now
I'm relying solely on you
Keep every ounce of strength
because I require the least drop
the pressure on you is immense

212

but don't collapse until I stop
There are two paths in sight
the long one has no end
the short is most enticing
but leave it, my body and friend
You'll get your reward
when you see what I can achieve
if you stick by me
I won't delude you or deceive
And when the fruits
are laid out for all to see
I'll finally let you rest
and lie down with me

(April 8th, 1989)

'The pressure on you is immense . . .' People with disabilities are often under psychological pressure to prove their worth in a society run largely by and for the able-bodied. This is not to minimise the contribution of those more enlightened 'abes'. It is a strange dichotomy that on the one hand there are low expectations of disabled people, because we are seen as ill or medical specimens, yet on the other hand some able-bodied people's expectations are too high and totally ignore the ramifications of a disability. Admittedly it is better to err on the demanding side but this may well entail guilt (albeit misplaced) or embarrassment in a disabled person at having to explain reasons for their inability to live up to those demands. I think explanations will continue to be necessary until disabled people are more integrated in society and able-bodied people are thus more aware too.

I like to ignore the medical aspects of my disability, such as pressure-sore prevention and chiropody care. They are indeed relatively minor aspects of my life but are still time-consuming enough to eat significantly into a working day. I am reluctant to mention the boring facts for fear of eliciting pity or illuminating a difference, but I want people to understand the demands on my life and

213

realise my time is limited in more senses than one. I wrote a poem for a friend with an invisible disability after a discussion when we attempted to explain the jumble of paradoxes in our lives. It is not a poetic masterpiece but has its place, all the same.

Same Difference

I want you to know me
without being nosey
I want you to question
without being inquisitive
I want you to understand
the delicate difference
while treating me the same
I want no allowances
while welcoming positive discrimination
I want no extra demands
while desiring equal expectation
I want you to get inside my skin
without my explanation

There are times when I simply want to go out as a human being, not as an educator, and I really do not want to feel forced to raise some stranger's consciousness. Often there are injustices it would be easier to ignore for fear of giving people with disabilities a bad name. I imagine it happening with the various travel agents and travel companies that I have dealt with, saying behind my back, 'Oh, disabled people always complain. We can never get it right so let's not bother.' If we are 'always complaining' it is because we have a lot to complain about! We are in a no-win situation. If we do not say anything things cannot improve, so I have to risk my reputation! The problem stems from the image of disabled people as passive recipients who should be eternally grateful for every crumb that comes their way. This is not an image I wish to perpetuate.

On my first day with Graeae a child commented after

seeing me, 'She's so happy.' The child's mother thought it was good that this was the impression I had left on a little girl. I was touched, but there should not be an onus on disabled people to be ultra-happy. Being sad is often not a lot to do with our disability and everything to do with our humanity. It therefore should not be the sole preserve of the able-bodied. Sometimes I have ended up feeling guilty if I am not happy whereas able-bodied people are allowed to feel as miserable as sin without being condemned for creating a bad impression. If I think about it I am generally of a sunny disposition, but sometimes a stream of mishaps makes it well-nigh impossible to remain bright.

For roughly a third of the year prior to this book's deadline I was without my 'normal' domestic back-up. That is, due to my two permanent assistants leaving at virtually the same time, I had temporary people working for me who were unfamiliar with my flat layout, filing system, food habits, etc. It was time-consuming constantly to explain every detail, as well as psychologically wearing. This is not to undermine the confidence or competence of the women concerned. Then, shortly before the completion of this book, I was struck down with a particularly vicious virus which entailed fainting and vile non-stop sickness. That and the ensuing weakness was sufficient to cope with alone, but the tailor-made loo seat bloke and the carpenter had disappeared without trace, so using the loo was tantamount to climbing Everest. For the length of time it took to make a new loo seat, I think they must have been growing the tree for the wood. I eventually got the old seat mended myself by a garage mechanic.

While the loo-seat saga was carrying on, the wheelchair was taken away with a question-mark hanging over its return date. For weeks, a special wheelchair cushion had been 'stuck in the post', my pricey pressure-sore prevention sheepskin was lost after a holiday and, to cap it all, the video broke down. I was too debilitated to feel anything much more than numb. If anyone had told me to be happy I would have replied with a quote on my wall. 'True happiness and spiritual joy does not mean living on a perpetual high, but may be compared to the ballast in a ship. With ballast the ship will roll in a storm, just as a person capable of true happiness and joy will feel pain in a crisis, but the storm will not capsize the boat which will quickly right herself even when struck by a wave. Similarly true happiness and spiritual joy does not mean living on a continuous high, unaffected by grief, sadness or loss, the pain of others, but it does mean we shall not sink into despair under the blows, but will recover peace and tranquillity when the storm is over.'

That quote was consoling when I first read it and has come to mean a great deal to me because I know I am not abnormal not to feel ecstatic seventy-five per cent of the time. My emotional chemistry makes me a person of peaks and troughs. In other words, I do feel things deeply and therefore experience acute pain, but I can also reach peaks of happiness which others are not capable of reaching. When I am in pain I want the space to express that pain. Through my expression it is exorcised and I become myself again.

I often feel a 'DO NOT WALLOW' pressure, particularly in London where people do not have the time to receive another's pain and therefore use this spoken or unspoken pressure as an excuse for their lack of ability to give. I wonder, what am I supposed to do? I do not want to be dishonest about myself but if I am afraid of alienating people by expressing the painful truth and worried about being thought self-pitying (an emotion I aim to avoid), my fear of misinterpretation and rejection cuts me off from the very human contact I require. It becomes a vicious circle and all my bottled-up sorrow will inevitably burst through and pour out in an exaggerated rush on the first poor victim I eventually communicate with properly. As Vera Brittain puts it in *Testament of Youth*: 'That's the worst of sorrow. It's always a vicious circle. It makes one tense and hard and disagreeable and this means that one repels and antagonises people and then they dislike and avoid one and that means isolation and still more sorrow.' One of my earliest poems was on this theme:

Whirlpool

Caught in a whirlpool of emotions
dragged down by my lack of control
I lashed out like an untrained beast
at those closest to me
I gave them blame instead of love
I couldn't pull myself out
but kicked blindly
at words meant kindly
nobody tried to discover why barbed arrows flew
when I never even strung the bow
then my hostility fought hostility
and drove away the comfort I sought
lost what I needed most
seeing the damage done
hating myself for hurting hostile friends
guilt made me avoid their company
left with no resources to make amends
I sank to the bottom
a sign said NO WAY OUT
in horror I realised I was there alone
    to swim to the top on my own
        a weak swimmer
            with weights attached
                at last found
                    air

now at the top of the whirlpool I can see through the
    mud
    but how can apology explain?
        I might get
            dragged down
                again

When I took part in a disability awareness training session for medical students, one bright young spark asked me what was the worst thing about being disabled. Maybe the most trying aspects are not the most obvious. Personally, it is the lack of spontaneity which is the thorn in my side. I even have to plan a hug so that I don't run over people's feet and ruin the moment of tenderness. The moment of tenderness might otherwise end up being the other person's little toe! An electric wheelchair, even of small dimensions like mine, can be sufficient literally to squash the most potent of passions. Friends of mine who have wised up to the weight in my wheels may step aside as they see me hurtling towards them, little knowing I only want to reach out to touch or hug. I then have to cover up my pain with the pretence that I was moving to do something else. Rosie recently pointed out a positive aspect of my wheelchair, which is my ability to create any desired space between myself and another person. Having a movable piece of furniture attached to me, I can seat myself as near or far as I want. Jim also noticed that people touch the wheelchair instead of me. It was a revelation and I thought, 'Yes they do touch it a lot. Great! It would be nice if they could handle touching me instead.' Thus I felt ambivalent relief towards my revelation. If the chair is an extension of me and people touch it as if it were close physical contact with me that's fine up to a certain point. The chair is so much a part of me but it is not ME.

Hug

as they enter the room
her heart expands
and wraps around their entire being
but they cannot see
or know what the shine
in her eyes is really meaning

so you who can must read her eyes
and respond to what they do
come down to her level
where she can reach to you

she hugs with her eyes
can you too?

It is very noticeable that disabled people do not receive as many platonic hugs as the able-bodied. A reason for this could be that people with disabilities are not seen as sexual beings and a hug is the same physical action whether it is sexual or platonic. The whole point of being demonstrative is to use non-verbal language, so it does not make sense to say, 'Come here. I want to give you a hug.' The magic moment is over before the sentence is finished.

The Door

The door
waiting
The wonder
cursing the metal
The trap
murdering spontaneity
The question
Will he?
Willing it to be
The gap
imagining the leap
eyes meet
my eyes speak
his eyes don't read
his eyes only see
arms by my side
but in my mind
thrown around his neck
Sacrificing my words

219

for his choice
Words have no place
Where limbs freely greet
Steeling my voice
not to seal the gap
with stupid nothings
too late
it's over
the test
the barrier
the door

The Church is not an improvement on worldly ways. Sadly, the reverse is true in my experience. One evening I was in a room full of a dozen people from my church who knew me and we were talking about openness. There was a good deal of discussion about the need to be open. I can't say I've ever found that a problem! After a while I poured out some of my pent-up pain and was surprised to find myself crying as I spoke of the need to be able to trust that people can take the load of your pain and the risk required if you are afraid of having the self-pity syndrome thrown in your face. I was not embarrassed at my tears but felt others were. However, it was not their embarrassment or lack of it that bothered me. What did hurt me was the lack of physical contact I received from a largely tactile group. One or two of the women responded but I had laid myself bare and not one person in the room came and gave me a healing hug. The men were happy to hug the able-bodied females hugely but even a small hug for a small person with a disability was sadly lacking.

I reminded myself of a poem I wrote in August 1988.

Leapfrog

I want to leap
into the arms
of every man I love

or ever loved
If I believed in reincarnation
I would be reborn a frog
but I will leap
eternally
in eternity
to make up for lost legs
These legs were made for leaping
and that's just what they'll do
One day these legs
will leap right up to you
I want to know
that you know
I want to leap

I sometimes think of that verse in the Bible which says God will not give us more than we can bear and I have often felt that muscular dystrophy would be my 'chosen' disability if everyone had to have one. I am quite a coward when it comes to physical pain so to have a disability which caused constant pain would be unbearable. On the other hand I could not have handled paralysis or no physical feeling. I could not cope with blindness or deafness due to the importance of music, and aural and visual communication and stimuli.

How significant that it was the International Year of Disabled People when I wrote to Rosie: 'Three vitally important things happened this year which I never thought would come true'. They were becoming an actress, achieving my independence by living away from home and not having to have injections. Only two years previously I had written in my *Muscular Dystrophy Journal* column of my 'impossible' ambition to become an actress, ending the piece 'How can I get anyone to accept me without a training, and how am I to get the training?' When I take a retrospective glance and compare my deepest desires with what I have done in reality I sit back in amazement, as if I am looking at the life of another person. It now seems incredible to me that I had my own flat in Aldershot where I got myself up and dressed, got to the loo, had a shower, got a taxi to work, cooked my own meals and so on, all without the use of a wheelchair and at an age when according to the medical profession I should have been dead. Admittedly it took time to manage around the flat on my own and I am no longer strong enough to do so. But at least I fulfilled my dream of independence and proved it was possible, even if the taxi drivers were rather taken aback when they opened the door and found me sitting on the floor!

'I want to branch out into singing and poetry . . . I've got so many ideas for poems and songs. I'd like to find musicians to work with and tour round giving recitals. My main ambition is to get a book of poems published,' to quote from an article written about me in *Buzz* in 1984. 'No doubt she'll do it,' wrote the journalist. I had forgotten I had stated my professional aims so precisely in print, but looking back five years later I can say I have lived up to the journalist's expectations exactly and accurately fulfilled my ambitions.

A number of people have said, 'you're too young to write your autobiography'. This is not the end of my 'story', but in the words of one of my favourite Melanie songs, 'Thank you life for having been'. I never expected my cup to be filled, but it's running over.

Ellen Wilkie died on 7th August 1989.